The Beauty of the Word

The Beauty of the Word

The Challenge and Wonder of Preaching

James C. Howell

WESTMINSTER
JOHN KNOX PRESS
LOUISVILLE • KENTUCKY

First edition
Published by Westminster John Knox Press
Louisville, Kentucky

11 12 13 14 15 16 17 18 19 20—10 9 8 7 6 5 4 3 2 1

Book design by Drew Stevens
Cover design by Pam Poll Design

Library of Congress Cataloging-in-Publication Data

Howell, James C.
  The beauty of the Word : the challenge and wonder of preaching / James C. Howell. — 1st ed.
      p. cm.
  Includes index.
  ISBN 978-0-664-23695-3 (alk. paper)
  1. Preaching. I. Title.
  BV4211.3H69 2011
  251—dc22

                                                                                2011004124

PRINTED IN THE UNITED STATES OF AMERICA

♾ The paper used in this publication meets the minimum requirements of the American National Standard for Information Sciences—Permanence of Paper for Printed Library Materials, ANSI Z39.48-1992

Westminster John Knox Press advocates the responsible use of our natural resources. The text paper of this book is made from 30% post-consumer waste.

Contents

Acknowledgments

Preaching is either a terribly lonely activity—you are really by yourself up there!—or the most corporate endeavor imaginable. People listen, or there is no preaching. Preachers read, we converse with others about being by yourself up there, we get tips at a Saturday night party, and we never prepare a single sermon without the curious chorus of voices that are our teachers, parents, friends, those who've loved us, and also those who've hurt us, some long dead and some we just passed in the hallway.

In my preaching life, to begin to name names is risky—in that it may never stop. But a few folks were kind enough to read part of this and offer some wise suggestions, such as Robert Moses, Suzanne Henderson, Laurie Clark, Richard Lischer, Tom Long, Dan Randall, and Dan Baughman. The latter two are among many students who've signed up for my preaching classes, and my ongoing collegiality with them and many others is one of the great privileges of my existence. I think of my colleagues on staff (staffs now) who have designed liturgies, selected music, led choirs, prayed, preached themselves, and offered me encouragement and the gift of friendship: Ellen Robison, George Ragsdale, Shane Page, Kevin Wright, Bill Roth, Jimmy Jones, Alisa Lasater, Steve James, Barbara Barden, Craig Kocher, Karen Easter, Kevin Turner, John-Palmer Smith, Shelly Webb, and Andy Baxter.

My family has quite ruggedly stuck with the peculiar regimen of sitting in a pew every week to hear the Word from dad, from husband—and I've then had the lovely experience of hearing one of my own children preach the Word. My in-laws have always been singularly encouraging, as have friends in ministry who've listened, even at a distance online, and been of personal support.

My real gratitude, and thus the dedication of this book, would be to the members of the four congregations that have over thirty years woken up on Sunday, gotten dressed, and filled pews and chairs, trusting me (at least most of them do!) to say something that matters, something beyond my pet thoughts but perhaps a Word from the Lord. The saints, believers, and seekers at Wesley Chapel in Misenheimer, Plaza in Charlotte, the Davidson Church, and Myers Park in Charlotte have filled my heart with much love and satisfaction as I look back (and still forward!) at the challenge and wonder of preaching, as together we contemplate the beauty of the Word.

Foreword

This provocative book, written by one of our generation's most creative pastors and preachers, is, in some ways, like an old and welcoming country house. It has a wide, generous, and comfortable front porch, where we are invited to sit for a spell in a rocker, pour a glass of lemonade, and join in on a wide-ranging, always fascinating, witty, and intellectually stimulating conversation about the ministry of preaching. There is storytelling and there is laughter. There is quiet and sometimes sad reflection, and there are joyful cries of discovery. There is shoptalk about illustrations and sermon delivery; there is encouraging talk about the importance of the preaching task, even in a culture blitzed by "messages" and churches sparsely filled with often distracted hearers; and there is candid confession about fear, failure, ambition, and bruising comments about sermons uttered at the church door.

But if we get up from the porch and go deeper into the house, we soon discover that this is not simply a book on preaching, no mere conversation about the making of sermons. This is also a book about being a faithful pastor, about how the ligaments of each Sunday's sermon are firmly attached to the larger frame of a pastor's life—to pastoral care, leadership, and the shepherding of God's people. Even more, it is a book about the whole of the Christian life, about walking faithfully in a world where the true paths are often hard to see and choked with weeds, about keeping one's eyes open to the light of Christ and, as Howell puts it, to "the grace of God getting its feet under real people down here."

James Howell is a scholar-pastor. He holds a Duke PhD in Old Testament studies, and he reads voraciously in theology, cultural analysis, and literature. His scholarship is evident on every page of this volume, but it never protrudes or calls attention to itself. His learning is always in the service of his pastoral practice, always strengthening his ministry to others. Howell reads and thinks and studies in order to sharpen his vision, and he does not want the reader to see who he is and what he has achieved nearly as much as he desires us to see what he *sees*.

So Howell wants all of us who preach to spend time in the study, to pore over the books and commentaries, but he refuses to let us stay there permanently. For Howell, serious sermon study and preparation are not about crafting sermons that beckon congregations to crowd into the minister's chambers but about sermons that move in the opposite direction, about sermons that find their way out in the world. Sermon study has centrifugal force, sending preachers out of their carpeted offices and onto the asphalt. The people who will hear us on Sunday, he writes, "have been in natural settings like an office tower, a factory, a bar, a movie theater, in the den watching TV, stalled in traffic; and if that is where they have lived, and if that is where we fantasize that they might someday know and connect with God, then perhaps we not only go to the same places, but even 'write' sermons there. Get outside, and do that talking out loud in a park or strolling downtown."

Preachers who seek wise counsel about how to prepare better sermons will not be disappointed in these pages. Howell has been an innovative and well-regarded preacher for many years. He has preached before countless congregations, in the halls of academic institutions, and on radio and television, and he has taught preaching at Duke and elsewhere. Like an experienced sailor, he has a firm working knowledge of how to set the homiletical jib sail and how to adjust the sermonic lines, and he generously shares his insights tempered by experience. For example, he knows the temptation of preachers to turn the Bible into a vanilla milkshake, blending and conflating discrete texts into an indistinguishable mixture, and he astutely warns us against this: "If you are preaching on Mark, do not veer off into Luke, and certainly not into Paul. If preaching on Isaiah, stick to Isaiah. Do not drift into Matthew!"

Or again, Howell knows the danger of trying to do too much in a single sermon. Some weeks, the preacher has gathered a whole basket of sermonic Easter eggs—a great story about something that happened at a homeless shelter, a terrific quotation from a novel, a penetrating insight about the text from a commentary, a fabulous thought gleaned from the op-ed page of the newspaper, a hilarious cartoon from the *New Yorker*. To include all of this and everything else the preacher has discovered in a single homily would inevitably produce a sermonic octopus with tentacles squirming in multiple directions. Howell urges homiletical restraint. A sermon with five or six units or "moves," is best, he advises, "which means you may have to jettison a lovely idea— or invest it in the bank for another day, another sermon." He goes on to say, "Most sermons I hear, including my own, try to do too much, and dump too much on the poor listener, who does not enjoy the benefit of seeing your manuscript or having sat with you throughout the agonizing preparation process."

There are many other examples of sage, on-the-ground practical advice about preaching to be found here, and this counsel is exceedingly valuable. The main contribution Howell makes to preachers, though, is to be found, I believe, in two striking themes that run through the whole book: pastoral imagination and the nature of the gospel.

In terms of pastoral imagination, Howell constantly dazzles the reader by what he is able to see in his mind's eye and by the connections he makes between the claims of the faith and everyday experiences of life. For example, the soliloquy of the rich fool in Jesus' parable, who muses that he might be able to solve a crisis in his life by pulling down his old barns and building bigger ones, leads Howell not into an excursus about first-century economics but into the suburban neighborhoods of his own city, where wealthy people are tearing down perfectly fine homes and building mansions on the lots, not because they physically need the space but because fragile egos need larger structures to be secure.

Or again, one day when Howell's five-year-old son interrupted him as he was busily working at the computer, Howell told him, "Son, you just have to get out of here; Dad has so much work to do." As his son dutifully trudged away, saying as he went, "OK, Daddy, I'll leave. I don't mean to annoy you," Howell realized what he had done, turned off the computer, and spent the day playing with his son. An ordinary moment in parenting? Perhaps, but by the time Howell is finished describing it, we have seen a truth about how God can use even the words of our children to call us out of our frenetic lives.

This kind of nimble joining of doctrine and life probably cannot be learned by mastering rules or sharpening techniques. As Augustine said of eloquence, it is first caught by imitation. This is one of the beauties of this book. We watch in amazement page after page as Howell weaves together the gospel and contemporary life. It is a marvelous dance to behold, the way Howell glides gracefully between the gospel and Main Street, and—miracle of miracles—by the end of the book, we are out on the dance floor ourselves, trying out the steps.

In addition to training our pastoral imagination, this book also gives us a fine gift in and through Howell's grasp of the profundity of the gospel. He is unfailingly critical of the tendency of the church and of Christians today to whittle down the gospel to manageable size, to domesticate the gospel so that it ends up being nothing more than a bland endorsement of our trivial aspirations and already in-place good intentions. "Did Jesus come to earth and nag people to be nice? Or to volunteer a little?" Howell asks. "No, Jesus spoke of the invasion of God into a world of people trying hard to be somewhat good, and that very world broke him, nailing him to a shaft of olive wood where he cried out that he had been forsaken by God."

This conviction about the invasive quality of the gospel leads Howell to sound what may be the most compelling warning in this book: "Do not write one more word of one more sermon until you have found something big and true to say; do not stand in a pulpit ever again unless you intend to speak of what is large, the fruit of good seeing and thinking, and with some urgency." At this point the reader wants to stand and applaud. In a culture where everything gets ground into easily digestible sound bites, Howell sounds the trumpet clearly, waking us up to the truth of the gospel's urgency and scope. Howell reminds us that the gospel is a word unlike other words, a word with some size!

Thomas G. Long
Candler School of Theology
Emory University

Introduction

1

Obligation and Inability

From the first time I preached, as a very idealistic but fidgety twenty-year-old, until just this past Sunday, having grayed now into my fifties, I have never shaken loose from the often-quoted thought of Karl Barth:

> We ought to speak of God. We are human, however, and so cannot speak of God. We ought therefore to recognize both our obligation and our inability and by that very recognition give God the glory. This is our perplexity.[1]

Perplexity I've had plenty of, and so has everyone else who has ever dared to stand in a pulpit. Yes, we have an obligation to preach. When I was a novice, that obligation felt rather noble, like the holy conflagration in Jeremiah's youthful soul: "There is in my heart as it were a burning fire shut up in my bones, and I am weary with holding it in" (Jer. 20:9). As I grow older, the obligation some days feels like being stuck. Yet if I shovel away the debris of weary routine, there are still smoldering embers underneath it all.

The obligation to speak of God, whether it feels like zealous passion or the numb inevitability of this week's calendar, is inextricably paired with an inability we know all too well. We go to refresher courses, read how-to books, mimic pulpit giants, fiddle with technique; but at the end of the day, at the end of every sermon, we sag a little, not having said quite enough, not precisely nailing the heart of the thing, sometimes even boring people, or (far worse!) merely entertaining them for a few diversionary minutes.

In a way this book is about failure in preaching, although I would defend homiletical failure as the only genuine sacrifice of words on the altar of God's Church. We'll talk about more than failure, including how preaching might miraculously work, the fascinating linkages between the prophetic sermon and the funeral homily, and what I call the "aftermath," how we feel when we sit down and field reactions. We will cover what we actually talk about, the way texts operate, where sermons happen (or don't happen), and how the whole constellation of tasks for which we are responsible and quirks that reside in our peculiar personalities might mingle and issue in something lovely, come Sunday.

But I do not think Paul was blowing smoke or being typically manipulative when he said he preached "in weakness and in fear and in much trembling" (1 Cor. 2:3). Homiletical giants write books that promise your sermons can be powerful and compelling; but Paul, without whom none of us would have jobs, said that his message was "folly" (1 Cor. 1:18), and that God's power is "made perfect in weakness" (2 Cor. 12:9). As Michael Knowles has put it, "For Paul the cruel death and unexpected resurrection of Jesus provide not only the *content* of his preaching, not merely the *means* by which preaching is made possible; they determine also the *manner* and the *method* by which he preaches."[2] In preaching we not only talk about powerlessness; we rather shamelessly put it on display. I am writing to invite us who preach to become weaker, to relish the folly, to thrive on our inability.

Preaching is an obligation, and we suffer an inability to do it well. Barth hatched his "obligation and inability" idea in a milieu that at least feels simpler than mine. Preaching has always been well-nigh impossible, but it simply must be harder now than ever. Nobody sees your robe or the degrees and ordination certificate on your office wall, and therefore grants you any authority. If anything, the opposite prevails: listeners are hungry for a word from the Lord, and yet they are poised to debunk. We preach to under-equipped deconstructors who read *The Da Vinci Code* or *The Shack* but never open a Bible; who surf the Internet and Google up spiritual answers; who have short attention spans and are frankly exhausted from their week long before you ever get cranking on your sermon; who are intrigued by other religions, other spiritualities, other diversions, other . . . well, anything other than what is old, tried, true, traditional. Gail Godwin has imagined an aging priest complaining to his grown daughter in words that explain well her novel's title, *Father Melancholy's Daughter*: "My ministry has been a stop-gap one. I came along too late, you see. The church I wanted to serve started crumbling a long time ago. . . . It's been my fate to preside over its final humiliations. Nobody gives a damn about symbols anymore."[3]

So much is made about preaching being tough in this postmodern, post-Constantinian, post-tried-everything world. But after we engage in a bit of appropriate self-pity, we probably had best recognize that preaching has always been tough, an uphill battle, against all odds, pressed to the margins. We find our multicultural milieu to be daunting; but Christianity was birthed, and somehow survived, in a world where Christians were fewer than 1 percent of the population for over a hundred years, and where the average Mediterranean city featured literally dozens of divinities worshiped by fawning crowds. Even in Old Testament times, when we might blithely assume everybody in Israel believed in God, the prophets declared God's Word—but theirs was what Walter Brueggemann calls "de-privileged testimony."

> It is de-privileged because it is the evidence offered by a community that is early nomads or peasants and that is late a community of exiles . . . a great distance from the great hegemonic seats of power and the great centers of intellectual-theological certitude. Israel always comes into the great courtroom of public opinion and disrupts the court, in order to tell a tale of reality that does not mesh with the emerging consensus that more powerful people have put together.[4]

Always. There never has been, and never will be, some sunny epoch when truthful preaching was or will be received with great zeal and passionate responsiveness. Preaching is hard, but that is why it is meaningful. Preaching is odd, unconfined, and unconfinable—hence its freedom.

And I can hardly blame my audience for homiletical short circuits. The burden is on me, on all of us; the inability would still be fully my own even if every person in the pew were savvy in Scripture, rigorous in prayer, fully formed by liturgy, and holy in lifestyle. They aren't, and I'm not either; so we adjust to these bare-knuckle facts and try to devise another sermon, acknowledging there is one and only one way to proceed: preaching does not depend on the cleverness, intelligence, or preparation of the preacher, but solely on the beauty, the inherent persuasiveness, of the One we proclaim. Not our persuasiveness, as we are shackled with inability, and not any kind of retro view of the authority of Scripture, but only the beauty of the Word stands a chance out there these days.

THE LYRE OF ORPHEUS

Frequently I contemplate a sermon the young Martin Luther King Jr. preached at Ebenezer Baptist Church, where his father was the pastor. "How the Christian Overcomes Evil" was punctuated by an illustration from mythology. The sirens sang seductive songs that lured sailors into shipwreck. Two, though, managed to navigate those treacherous waters successfully, and King contrasted their techniques. Ulysses stuffed wax into the ears of his rowers and strapped himself to the mast of the ship, and by dint of will he managed to steer clear of the shoals. But Orpheus, as his ship drew near the sirens, simply pulled out his lyre and played a song more beautiful than theirs, so his sailors listened to him instead of to them.[5]

Every preacher knows how it feels to grit her teeth in labor, to strive valiantly to keep his rowers with him, just to survive to preach another day, to keep the Church afloat. We slam the office door and grope about for something to strap ourselves on to. We may declare resolutely that the Bible is inspired, that truth is revealed only in Scripture, and so we cram that Word into their ears. Or we fumble across the bookshelf and finger a thick commentary, place it next to the latest collection of "catchy illustrations," hoping some invisible magnetism sparks some arc we can type into the computer, for time is pressing and we have to get to the hospital—although we would prefer to get outside in the sunshine for a while.

But think about Orpheus. Calmly, deploying some simple artistry, Orpheus trusted the beauty of the song, and he played. Frankly, if the preacher wants to be "effective" (and later we will have to examine how we can fall into a dark hole and never "get it" if this is our sole objective), we have to reckon with the harrowing truth that most Church people nowadays won't let you stuff anything in their ears. They could care less if you are tied to the mast of all those slogans we fall back on, like "The Bible is the Word of God," or "The Church is of God," or whatever we say Baptism or scriptural Christianity requires.

If we are to persuade, if we are to give voice to the mysteries of God, then we must take quite seriously the task of picking up the lyre and playing the song in ways that are lovely, although perhaps in the way a young semitalented guitar player might woo his lover, the sincerity and courage of the attempt compensating for lack of talent. St. Augustine urged preachers to marshal their rhetoric, "to teach, to delight, and to persuade. . . . When he does this properly he can justly be called eloquent, even though he fails to win the assent of his audience,"[6] although Augustine clearly believed all preachers could persuade and win assent.

By temperament and training, I have tended to preach like Ulysses, strapping myself to some mast (the inspiration of Scripture? the authority of the Church?) and straining to shut out the voice of evil, forgetting that we have this beauty, that God may be thought of as Beauty. Christendom has plenty of beauty: our buildings (whether a historic cathedral like Chartres or the little wooden A-frame my grandfather and his friends built with their own hands after strong winds huffed and puffed and blew the old Church down, both things of beauty perhaps in the way a child's coloring and a Rembrandt are both very much "art"), our liturgy (whether Cranmer's elegance or the rhythm of an African chant), the music (in its dizzying diversity), stained glass, sculpture, the lilt of spring's first flower, the face in the mirror.

So why does so much of our talk veer toward ugliness? In my preaching I have railed against various woes: I attack society's decadent pleasures with a Scrooge-like sourness. I attack war with a verbal violence. I say, "You should pray, you should serve the poor, you should be holy," unwittingly conjuring up in my listeners' minds memories of some battle-ax schoolteacher wagging a chagrined finger. The singer Jewel, in "I'm Sensitive," after noting that if we're told we're bad that's the only idea in our heads, hauntingly suggests,

> But maybe if we are surrounded in beauty,
> someday we will become what we see.

What is beauty? Scholars who write about aesthetics often quote Rilke ("Beauty is the beginning of terror"), but for my money I prefer Elaine Scarry's image:

> You are about to be in the presence of something life-giving, life-saving. It is not clear whether you should throw yourself on your knees before it, or keep your distance, but you had better figure out the right answer because this is not an occasion for carelessness or leaving your posture to chance. It is not that beauty is life-threatening, but instead that it is life-affirming.[7]

The Church is an ark of the covenant that bears beautiful words that matter. The Church is a manger, and swaddled inside is Jesus—the one about whom we sing, "Fairest Lord Jesus, Beautiful Savior." Something life-giving, life-saving: it really is unclear whether to kneel or run, but you have to look.

Through an unlikely chain of circumstances, I found myself at a gathering of Pentecostal clergy, and during worship I noticed the man next to me drift away from the crowd, his hands lifted, gazing somewhere beyond the ceiling, repeating over and over, "O Jesus, you are so beautiful. O Jesus, you are so beautiful." What is that? We more frequently go at Jesus with the latest deal we're working on, asking him to add his leverage to our agenda. "Jesus, can you help my back stop hurting? Can you make my spouse more responsive? Can you hold off on the rain until the picnic is over?" How many light years is this paltry religiosity from the compelling loveliness of a man gasping, "O Jesus, you are so beautiful"? Was he a great orator? I don't know, I don't care. He played the lyre and I was entranced.

Can I be like Orpheus and trust the beauty of the Savior? I can adamantly say true things about the teaching authority of the Church or the Scriptures being God's Word, but do such truths stand a chance in our destabilized intellectual culture? Isn't our best, truest chance simply to let the beauty be itself, and allow Fairest Lord Jesus, Beautiful Savior, to draw people to himself?

HIS BEAUTY IS OUR DEFORMITY

What is our song? Jesus did not come down as a mighty warrior, unleashing a divine juggernaut to crush his foes. Jesus came as an infant. When my oldest was born, I took her to the Church where blue-collar laborers, men with gruff voices, melted at the sight of her, their voices cooing with sweet peeping sounds, their massive hands become gentle pillows holding her. Jesus, nursing at Mary's breast: how beautiful. Why did the fishermen drop their nets and traipse off after a guy they had just met? Wasn't there something compelling, something beautiful about him? This Jesus was gentle with those who had been roughed up by life: lepers, prostitutes, tax collectors. How beautiful. His teaching: instead of "Blessed are the rich, the cool, the good-looking," he said, "Blessed are the poor, blessed are those who mourn, blessed are the merciful, blessed are the peacemakers." How beautiful.

But some didn't think so. They arrested this beautiful Savior and executed him, nailing him to an olive shaft: the zenith of ugliness. And yet St. Augustine, contemplating the crucifixion, wrote that "His deformity was our beauty."[8] The very beauty of God, hidden and revealed simultaneously in the cross.

Why does this beauty matter? Because, despite our wariness, we all want to give the fragile crystal of ourselves away to what is truly beautiful. Because we laugh, we cry, we dream, we long to be moved. Listen to this marvelous thought from Stanley Hauerwas:

> We must be attracted by a beauty so compelling we discover lives not our own. Such a discovery comes through suffering and takes time, because we do not give up our illusions easily. Liturgy is quite literally where we learn to suffer God's beauty and so suffering discover we are made in God's image. Through worship we discover the truth about ourselves, making possible lives of goodness otherwise impossible. The beauty, the goodness, and the truth of our liturgy is tested by our being sent forth. If we are not jarred by the world to which we return, then something has gone wrong. The beauty we have beheld in the gift of God's Son leaves its mark. Formed by such beauty we no longer desire to live by the lies that would have us call lies true, evil good, and ugliness beautiful.[9]

We have seen the beautiful Savior, and we won't even notice the door slamming behind us as we drop our nets and traipse off after him, mostly listening to his Orphean song, our only words to him being either "Jesus, you are so beautiful," or something like "I'm sensitive; I've seen enough ugliness; show me your loveliness." Maybe if we are surrounded in beauty, someday we will become what we see.

How does a sermon become that more beautiful song? Is it even possible? Having preached for more than half of my life now, I recognize how many of my sermons have been rather pedestrian, flat-footed, sound enough theologically and exegetically, but falling with a bit of a thud. But then there are moments when I feel as if that lyre is in my hands, and listeners miraculously overhear the music that truly is beautiful, the truth that is mesmerizing, even if only for a few moments in the middle of all my verbiage, despite my fumblings. So I am writing to think about how and why this happens, how it might happen again for me and for you.

This is in no way a "How to preach beautiful sermons" book that, if you only read and put it into practice, you can sail smoothly into calm waters. Instead, I want us to reflect together on the subject of preaching, with some personal ruminations and theological suggestions tying what we do in the pulpit to how we run the Church and live our personal lives. I want us to learn what I still hope to learn before I'm too old to preach any longer: that failure is embraceable, that broken-ness has its peculiar loveliness, and that what I've been missing in my dogged determination to succeed and preach effectively is precisely the grace of God, which I talk about but never quite acknowledge. If any of this is helpful, encouraging, or a prod to the imagination, then we can be grateful to God. If it isn't, we still have to figure out how to negotiate the perilous rocks without strapping anybody to any masts or stuffing wax in anybody's ears.

The Subject Matters

2

What to Talk About

So how do we decide what exactly to talk about come Sunday (or come Wednesday or Thursday or Saturday night when we're actually writing)? In this section I want to explore the ways we select what we will say and the way we handle a given text. What is a text anyway? How does a text do its work (and thus how does a sermon on a text try to mimic that work)? How do we manage to say things that are truthful, full of truth, or at least not full of BS or riddled by semitruths? Where do sermons happen, from the preparer's viewpoint? In the office? In a bar?

I prepare, preach, read, and listen to a lot of sermons—my own, those of colleagues and folks who are kind enough to share with me or even ask for some conversation on our mutual displays of inability and obligation. Most suffer, when they suffer, from some sort of shrinkage of subject, a narrowing of what we talk about; or it's all just a bit flat, superficial, or obvious. When we address people who bother sitting through a sermon, we need to grapple with their deepest dreams, wounds, and secrets. The preacher's fantasy should be that anyone paying attention might say of the preacher what Roberta Flack sang about a singer she heard:

> Strumming my pain with his fingers,
> Singing my life with his song,
> . . . .
> Telling my whole life with his words . . .
> I felt he found my letters, and read each one out loud.

We haven't read their letters, we don't know their whole lives. Or do we? I know you, you know me, we share this deep common humanity; we are all of us lonely, unsure of ourselves, clinging to what we've marshaled for ourselves, dreaming absurdly grand dreams, sad though and a little bit numb lately, wishing that something else, something or somebody new, would come around the corner and life would no longer be on hold. We are full of good intentions, we mess up, we are weary, we love.

But the sermon isn't really a robust diagnosis of human nature, essential as it will prove to be to strum people's pain with our fingers and kill them rather softly with a sermon that's just a sermon. What we talk about is even bigger—and that's saying a lot: bigger than the astonishing length, depth, and complexity of my life, and yours, and everybody else's. We get to talk about what is way too massive, or too microscopic, for mere words. We speak of God. We worry too much about our style or whether we've studied enough, but really it's the mind-boggling subject matter that makes or breaks the sermon. Assessing the wisdom and eloquence of Abraham Lincoln's speeches, Adam Gopnik suggests this:

> Writing well isn't just a question of winsome expression, but of having found something big and true to say and having found the right words to say it in, of having seen something large and having found the right words to say it small, small enough to enter an individual mind so that the strong ideas of what the words are saying sound like sweet reason. Good writing is mostly good seeing and good thinking, too. It involves a whole view of life, and making that view sound so plausible that the reader adheres to it as obvious before he knows that it's radical. . . . Our heroes should be men and women possessed by the urgency of utterance, obsessed by the need to see for themselves and to speak for us all.[1]

Do not write one more word of one more sermon until you have found something big and true to say; do not stand in a pulpit ever again unless you intend to speak of what is large, the fruit of good seeing and thinking, and with some urgency.

When we scramble to get a sermon together, we latch far too quickly onto something neat, cute, catchy—but far too trivial to bear the weight of truth. Anything that can be e-mailed to you, all of those cute, sweet little anecdotes that are easily remembered and that might appear on a flowery poster: do not repeat such banalities; they are too small, they cannot carry the freight, they are too obvious, too thin. Not only should we hit the delete button at the sight of anything that isn't big enough: we also need to avoid like the plague any thoughts that are simplistic perversions of the Gospel, no matter how much listeners might nod with recognition and approval. Thomas Merton told of going off to school at Oakham and hearing the chaplain's finest sermon. The text? First Corinthians 13:

> His exegesis was a bit strange. "Charity" simply stood for "all we mean when we call a chap a 'gentleman.'" In other words, charity meant good-sportsmanship, cricket, the decent thing, wearing the right kind of clothes, using the proper spoon, not being a cad. "A gentleman is patient, is kind; a gentleman envieth not . . ." And so it went. The boys listened tolerantly to these thoughts. But I think St. Peter and the Apostles would have been rather surprised at the concept that Christ had been scourged and beaten by soldiers, cursed and crowned with thorns and finally nailed to the Cross and left to bleed to death in order that we might all become gentlemen.[2]

Merton's reference to St. Peter and the Apostles is itself interesting. Which apostle do we preach at any given moment? Do we preach a single text? Anyone who's officiated at a wedding can well understand how 1 Corinthians 13, lifted out of Paul's longer letter to Corinth, and out of the context of the larger New Testament witness to Christ who was beaten and scourged, can become a vapid rumination on that mood modern people misname "love." To say big things about a big subject, how do we do so, given the strictures of the text at hand?

THE TEXT AS A CASTLE WINDOW

Why do we even mention that a text might have something like "strictures"? Seminary professors, with shrewd intent, instruct prospective preachers to stick to the text at hand. *If you are preaching on Mark, do not veer off into Luke, and certainly not into Paul. If preaching on Isaiah, stick to Isaiah; do not drift into Matthew! Let the Old Testament stand on its own!* And with good reason. The preacher must hear the text for what it is, and not rush prematurely to some pet text that is more congenial to what the preacher would really like to say this morning. I have taught this approach myself, and have upbraided preachers for waltzing too swiftly away from the text at hand. Dietrich Bonhoeffer, writing from a Nazi concentration camp cell in 1943, quite famously warned us not to leap so quickly to the New Testament:

> My thoughts and feelings seem to be getting more and more like those of the Old Testament. It is only when one knows the unutterability of the name of God that one can utter the name of Jesus Christ; it is only when one loves life and this earth so much that without them everything seems to be over that one may believe in the resurrection; it is only when one submits to God's law that one may speak of grace. It is not Christian to want to take our thoughts and feelings too directly from the New Testament.[3]

But I find myself worrying less about dancing from one portion of Scripture to another than about our proclivity to dance from the text to whatever pet thoughts we happen to harbor about the universe. I wonder if it might even help the preacher to keep the sermon's subject framed within the treasury of Scripture if she actually were expected not only to talk about the pericope of the day, properly exegeted, but actually to lead listeners down another lovely hallway or two within the broader biblical witness itself.

Yes, exegesis of the primary text at hand is indispensable, and if you have rambled through the Hebrew or Greek with a commentary or two, you've used up a lot of precious time already. But what if the sermon could be informed by a rigorous kind of exegesis, but not itself wind up as a mere report of the exegesis, and of only this text and no other? Why should the preacher pretend, if considering Isaiah, that Matthew somehow does not exist? Didn't Matthew himself tie up threads from Isaiah, and Mark, and the Psalms, to weave a full tapestry depicting the wonder of Christ? Did the Church not survive and thrive while hearing the homilies of Augustine, Chrysostom, Luther, Calvin, Wesley, and Spurgeon, preachers who without apology ranged all over the canon of Scripture?

What if the preacher were not confined by a single text, but were liberated by that very text to roam wide-eyed throughout the entire Bible? And not then bumping up against the canon of Scripture as a fence, but leaping beyond to see the glory of Scripture as played out in the drama of God's Church throughout the ages? And even then, not stopping until taking wing and soaring into the tangible life of the world this very minute, letting the melody of God's beauty pluck the chords of my life, my parishoners' lives, the loveliness of God nestling between the couple holding hands, embracing the grieving widow, racing through the frightened mind of the manic depressive, applying a healing balm onto shamed memories, resurrecting stone dead hearts, rifling through broken relationships and cold thoughts devoid of compassion, rising up on the wings of the morning, elevating the congregation gradually from the words of a simple text into the beautiful presence of God?

Imagine this. Instead of narrowly focusing on just the single, framed text for the day, we might think of a given text as a window into the broader reality of our faith, of the kingdom of God, one more window into the heart of God. Imagine coming upon a grand castle. From one angle you admire its towers. Walking closer, you notice the light glinting off its windows. You peek through one window, then another, then another. Over time, looking through many windows, you experience more of the castle, its furnishings, its grandeur, the life transpiring within. A given Sunday's text is a unique window; only this window yields this viewpoint on the treasures of the castle.

A sermon on a text could be conceived in this way: you gather up your friends and lead them out to the castle, crowding around one of its windows. You look, you explore the day's text, which is nothing more than a window. Later on, you guide them around to another window, and point out more of the wonders of the castle. A given window is interesting, but only briefly, for the window invites us to look inside. The preacher, then, need not focus only on a single window, but can dare to move about the canon of Scripture, while still relishing the peculiar perspective through that one window. Today's passage is not confining, but liberating. The mystery of the heart of God is exponentially larger than a single text, and the preacher is then freed over a season of sermons to show how the rooms interconnect and become not merely stone walls with windows, but actually a warm home inside.

Or perhaps we can reverse the image. In Elizabeth von Arnim's terrific 1922 novel, *The Enchanted April*, a woman notices a peculiar ad in the paper: "To those who appreciate Wistaria and sunshine. Small medieval Italian castle on the shores of the Mediterranean to be let furnished for the month of April. Box 1000, The Times." She can't get it out of her mind, for she is a woman bound to husband, home, duty; "she stayed happy by forgetting happiness." She, like many people to whom we preach, and like many of us who do the preaching, has gone on "being good for so long you get miserable." So she gets a friend to go with her. They arrive at night, in pouring rain and howling winds; fearing for their lives, they wish they had not come. But then, in the morning, she wakes up and opens the shutters:

All the radiance of April in Italy lay gathered together. The sun poured in on her, the sea lay asleep in it, hardly stirring, across the bay lovely mountains, the wall of the castle, flower-starred slope. She stared. Such beauty; and she there to see it, and she alive to feel it. Her face was bathed in light, lovely scents caressed her, a tiny breeze gently lifted her hair. Not to have died before this, to have been allowed to see, breathe, feel this—her lips parted. But what could one say? It was as though she could hardly stay inside herself, it was as though she were washed through with light. How astonishing to feel this sheer bliss. . . . At home she had been so good and merely felt tormented. Now she had taken off all her goodness and left it behind her like a heap of rain-sodden clothes; and she only felt joy. She was stripped of goodness, and exulting. The familiar words of the Great Thanksgiving came quite naturally into her mind, and she found herself blessing God for her creation, preservation, but above all of God's inestimable Love—out loud, in a burst of acknowledgment.[4]

Preaching may just be stripping people of their goodness, and opening shutters so they might exult in a burst of acknowledgment. Perhaps the preacher needs to be stripped of homiletical goodness as well . . . and learn to exult.

STRIPPED OF GOODNESS AND EXULTING

Inability and even failure in the pulpit need not be despised, but can be befriended as an unwanted but much needed stripping of goodness. So many sermons urge people to be good. The majority of them—while occasionally pasting God on the outside—are really about us doing better, being better, trying harder, and there is no grace, and thus no joy, in me or in the people who are afflicted with this diet of preaching. What is the Gospel, anyway? Did Jesus come to earth and nag people to be nice? Or to volunteer a little? No, Jesus spoke of the invasion of God into a world of people trying hard to be somewhat good, and that very world broke him, nailing him to a shaft of olive wood where he cried out that he had been forsaken by God. Not many sermons actually make it to the cross, and I do not mean the glib declaration that because of the cross we aren't in as much trouble as we thought we were. The cross is God's ultimate embrace of brokenness, the enfleshing of the kind of love that does not even attempt to alter anybody else, but simply loves.

What did Paul say? We are children of God, and heirs of the very riches of heaven, "provided we suffer with him" (Rom. 8:17). Sermons dote on the children of God idea, and occasionally tantalize us with the fantasy of heavenly riches; but we do not wish to raise the unpleasant specter of suffering. Oh, we may give a nod to Christ's suffering, but suggesting that because he suffered we don't have to. Yes, Jesus died, and so you're not really in any trouble at all; so can the guilt, go about your life, and be happy.

But Paul said, not just here but throughout his letters, echoing what the prophets and saints have tried to tell us: "provided we suffer with him." Suffering is not a dark place away from which we rush to get close to God where all is sunny. Suffering is where God is. Brokenness is the inevitable precondition for grace. The Gospel isn't God's stellar effort to make your life smooth, healthy, and happy. Were it otherwise, the centurion could never have looked on the ravaged, bloodied corpse of Jesus and declared, "Truly this man was the Son of God!" (Mark 15:39): this one, not the smiling, finely robed, laughing, healthy one, but this one, sacred head now wounded, fairest Lord Jesus.

Why then do we preach sermons on banal topics like "How God Helps You Reduce Stress" or "How to Have a Happy Marriage" or "How to Make our City a Nicer Place"? Pagans are frankly better at these topics than we are; and if we attend to the Scriptures, we see a stunningly different plot unfolding. Jeremiah is close to God, and dares to follow and give voice to God's messages, and he winds up isolated and sorrowful. The first Christians were ostracized in business and made a laughingstock in their neighborhoods. Jesus was homeless, rejected, and died a gruesome death.

Yet it is this bizarre, paradoxical beauty that people just might hear if we let it be said. And this chiaroscuro message, this paradox that does not blush in the face of pain, this mystery that ushers us when we cannot fix anything into joy itself, has the peculiar advantage of being true, or not merely true, but truth itself. At the end of the day, you have to decide that the people probably suspect that blithe self-help projects will fail, because they know they need more help than the self can give. Somewhere in their hearts, if we unstop their ears and simply play the song, the truth God wove into the very design of the universe enjoys a surprising allure; and in the shedding of our goodness we just might discover what we were desperately hungry for, the grace of God that seems to dawn only on those who are stressed, broken, unhappy, and in places that are not so very nice, and always and only through that opened window where we are stripped of our goodness.

More on that later. For now let us simply say that we might dig into the library and reread Augustine, or Luther, or whatever that seminary professor was trying to tell us about the mystery of God, the hiddenness of God, the atonement, the cause for which martyrs gave their lives—a cause surely much nobler than stress reduction. In terms of preaching this Gospel, which wasn't devised by Luther or Augustine but by God Almighty, we may need to relearn how to be attentive to texts. So let us turn back to the texts, our windows into (or out of!) the castle of God's inestimable Love. How do we get these things to open? How do texts work?

3

How Texts Work

Every week, every preacher attempts a daring leap from some text or another to a sermon. No matter how well trained, widely read, or rhetorically agile the preacher might be, the leap is scary. Unless the preacher has caved to the banality of ministry and is simply going through the motions, the pressure is intense for the sermon to "work," to get something accomplished—but what? For people to give more money? To convert the unconverted (who are more likely out fishing than eager to hear a word from the Lord)? For the preacher to be liked?

We can devise superb goals for preaching. My personal favorites are "to glorify God" and "the transformation of the Body of Christ." But how can a sermon achieve something so dramatic? How does a sermon actually work? or fail to work? We habitually domesticate the untamable vivaciousness of the text, transmuting a text that must have been marvelous or startling before it became a text into some sort of soporific, boring our listeners (and perhaps ourselves). How can a sermon work? and not be predictably dull?

It could be that we pay too much attention to the sermon and not enough to the text. Yes, we are nagged by our interiorized homiletical monitor: stick to the text; trust the text; the sermon isn't you and your fondest, most pious thoughts, but a proclamation of the text. But the pressure is still on the sermon, isn't it? I stare at the text, perhaps I read it aloud, I sift through a commentary or two, I attend my lectionary group. I try to find a point to the text, or something that looks

21

promising—and then I'm off, writing down ideas, cutting and pasting, maybe practicing on Saturday. Then Sunday comes, and goes—and another text lies in wait. I pay attention to the texts, but does the *sermon* work? How is it that the text, which sparked a riot in the first century, elicits yawns in the twenty-first?

What if we pay less attention to whether the sermon works, and more to whether the *text* works—or, since we are obliged to believe that texts work, *how* the text works? How, after all, do texts work? Texts *were* sermons before they became texts *for* sermons. A handful of Christians huddled in Philippi and heard Paul's parchment letter read aloud: "Have this mind among yourselves . . ." (Phil. 2:5). A few dozen believers tried to find a quiet place in bustling Antioch to hear the Gospel—quite literally, the Gospel of Matthew—read out loud in a single sitting: "Blessed are the poor in spirit . . ." (Matt. 5:3). In ancient Israel, travelers in ragged caravans were encouraged on their way to Mount Zion by songs they had recited and sung since childhood: "How lovely is thy dwelling place . . ." (Ps. 84:1). These great texts worked. No sermon needed to be attached. The texts *were* sermons, they stood quite well on their own as God's words. And they converted people, they transformed the people of God and eventually the Body of Christ, and a scintillating movement was set in unstoppable motion by the way these texts worked in those who heard them.

Frankly, some texts must work even better today than they did when they first were sermons. Examples abound, but my favorite must be Luke 12:16–20:

> "The land of a rich man brought forth plentifully; and he thought to himself, 'What shall I do, for I have nowhere to store my crops?' And he said, 'I will do this: I will pull down my barns, and build larger ones; and there I will store all my grain and my goods. And I will say to my soul, Soul, you have ample goods laid up for many years; take your ease, eat, drink, be merry.' But God said to him, 'Fool! This night your soul is required of you; and the things you have prepared, whose will they be?'"

In my city we have a startling number of perfectly fine homes for sale, but we dub them "tear-downs," as they are bought, razed, and replaced by huge domiciles that in turn put pressure on the little house next door to go up for sale and be torn down as well. When Jesus told the parable, I can imagine a few guys standing around who wanted to construct bigger barns; but in the twenty-first century, when our obsession is more and bigger, the story with absolutely no explanation whatsoever tears down our restless arrogance and craving for ever grander structures that might bolster a fragile ego in search of security.

Of course, the preacher can't just read the text and sit down, tempting as that strategy might be. We have to say something, something that will work. But what? When we are confronted by one of those texts that used to be a sermon before it became a text for a sermon, the question to ask is always "How does the text work?" and not "How will the sermon work?" In fact, the sermon that works best is the sermon that is in sync with the way the text works.

Too many sermons work against the way the text works. Consider Jesus' story about a father who had two sons. How many sermons, in response to an imaginative story full of drama and heart, become didactic lessons about living or the abstract nature of divinity? "There are four points to Luke 15:11–32"—or maybe there are three? or five? There are no "points" to a story, any more than there is a "point" to a painting or a poem. We feel some urge to tie the text up in a nice little bow, so people will ooh and aah at our preaching prowess: the sermon seemingly should have a digestible morsel, a single thrust, a neat zinger ending. But Jesus didn't zing anybody with a good ending to this story—or to any of his stories, for that matter. Did the prodigal son get things ironed out and become a solid family man? Did the older brother come in to the party and hug the one who was lost and then found? We do not know. Jesus left it dangling. He opened a wild, risky vista of possibilities; he threw open a window into the very heart of God—and then, evidently, just let his listeners think, reflect, perhaps converse together, ruminate, scratch their heads, and wonder, "What on earth could be next?"

The story works because of its lingering incompleteness, and the sermon on this text should never be diagrammable or chartable, and the sermon should never exhibit closure. There are not four or five or three items to enumerate—but a heart or two might be broken, an unanswerable question might drift around for a lifetime, an imagination or two might be expanded. The sermon on this text paints a tentative portrait of an alternate universe, and when the preacher turns to sit down, the people in the pews might object at first to the lack of a neatly packaged little lesson to it all, but then in the rippling wake of the boat rowing away, the buoyant feel of riding the tide of the way of Jesus in the world will pull the Body toward new life.

But not all texts work the same way, so the preacher can never settle on a formula for how to approach texts. If the sermon works the way the text works, then a sermon on an epistle will work very differently from one on a Psalm or a saga out of Israel's hazy past.[1] "Narrative preaching" was in vogue for quite some time—but could there be such a thing as "Poetic preaching," or "Wisdom preaching," or "Epistolatory preaching"? If the text (that was something of a sermon before it became a text for a sermon) is a psalm of praise, such as the eloquent Psalm 8, the sermon could speak directly to God, couldn't it? "O God, I stood out in the dark last night and envied the Israelites, whose skies were darker, and therefore brighter. They could see clearly what the ambient light from the mall and office buildings blotted out for me. But I know that the heavens are still telling your glory, I know from the Hubble telescope some of the fantastic grandeur of space that seems infinite only from my small perspective. I feel so small down here. But you came down! You loved us too much to leave us on our own in this massive place with shiny things. You are mindful of me, of us, and I am in awe. I am comforted—or I should say *we* are comforted. We are stunned. You tenderly care for us, together . . ."

If the text is a Wisdom saying, such as Proverbs 23:31–32 ("Do not look at wine . . . when it sparkles in the cup and goes down smoothly. At the end it bites like a serpent, and stings like an adder"), then the sermon has every good reason to be didactic.[2] You embody the spirit of the ancient sage, you furrow your brow, perhaps you even wag a loving finger, and you instruct the young in the ways of goodness.

UNPREDICTABILITY

Once we become attentive to the way texts work, we notice the shock value in virtually every text. Onlookers did not listen to the first texts that were sermons before they became texts for sermons and blithely nod in bland agreement with the conventional wisdom of the followers of Jesus. Listeners were puzzled, and riots broke out. "These men who have turned the world upside down have come here also" (Acts 17:6). "The word of the cross is folly . . ." (1 Cor. 1:18). Jesus said "You have heard that it was said, 'You shall not commit adultery.' But I say to you . . ." (Matt. 5:27–28). Jesus took texts that had themselves been sermons and twisted them into something shocking, with a "but I say to you." Every sermon—every sermon!—should be a surprise. The worst sermon is the predictable sermon, because the Gospel is not the epitome of predictability. For the sermon to work the way the text works, the preacher is vigilant to notice the startling angle of the text. And it is at that point of the text's oddness that the people of God become transformed into a holy oddness. It is the "but I say to you" moment that becomes the metamorphosis.

Listeners may have heard many of these texts before. They may well have heard sermons on these texts before. So, at all costs, the preacher must know where people think the preacher is going—and steadfastly refuse to go there. Suppose the reading is Luke 10:29–37, the duly famous parable of the Good Samaritan. The reader begins, and people tune out—the way frequent flyers pay no attention whatsoever to the flight attendant who is reviewing the safety and emergency procedures before the plane takes off. Where do they think you're going with this text? They yawn and wait for the pedestrian lesson: "So often you're like the priest or the Levite, in such a rush, hurrying right past the poor person who needs help. But God wants you to be like the Samaritan. Slow down, help the guy who's beaten and bleeding by the side of the road." They are snoring by now, or rifling in their minds through the afternoon's to-do list.

Maybe the predictable sermon is more nuanced, with some modern parallels to today's Samaritans: "Jews and Samaritans loathed one another; we have our Samaritans, don't we? People with AIDS? Immigrants? The poor (or rich) person across the tracks? Jesus wants us to love them." Like the priest and Levite, the bored pew sitters quite justifiably rush right past the poor bleeding sermon lying by the side of the road.

So what shall we do with the Good Samaritan text? You may not know just yet, but you firmly make a vow to yourself: "Whatever I say this Sunday, it will not be the predictable or the trite." It may well be a superb idea to help people who are hurting or to reconcile with strangers. But when Jesus told the story, it wasn't an old saw. People who heard him left home and family to follow him, risked life and limb to proclaim him. In fact, at the end of the day, Luke 10:29–37 is about this one they left home and family to follow. Jesus is the teller of the story, and that must matter. It's not a free-floating story Confucius or Plato might have told. It's from the mind and heart of Jesus, and the story is in full harmony with who he was.

In hatching sermons we can reconsider what I call the "identification game." We hear a Bible story, and we begin to identify with some character or another—understandably, and even helpfully. But we don't play around with the possibilities thoroughly enough. With the parable of the Good Samaritan, the option seems to be priest/Levite or Samaritan. But what about the bloodied victim by the side of the road? Don't listeners know what that feels like? What about the guys who beat him up in the first place? Whom have we hurt, even if unwittingly?

These are questions with energetic potential in the preparation of a sermon. But the better questions are always about Jesus, the teller of the story—or by extension, about God, the subject of not just the sermon, but the subject of all subjects. Wasn't Jesus beaten and bloodied? Wasn't Jesus the one who spared no effort in helping a stranger? Isn't Jesus the stranger? How do texts work? These texts that were sermons before they became texts for sermons are about God, and they work because they point us toward God. Contemplating the macabre but theologically beautiful painting of the crucifixion by Matthias von Grünewald, which features John the Baptist with a long, bony, crooked finger pointing to the dying Jesus, Karl Barth said, "I want to be that finger."

The sermon that works points to Jesus crucified, foolishness to the wise eyes of the world. This is why every sermon must resist the temptation to echo the conventional wisdom of the world. One Thanksgiving I heard a sermon that rather humorously yet adamantly declared that it is good to be grateful. Two patients lay in a hospital room. One expressed gratitude to the nurses, aides, physicians, and visitors; the other griped, whined, complained about the food, rang the nurses repeatedly with impossible demands. The sermon's clinching point? "It is good to be grateful." And so it is. But the sermon failed to work— or it "worked" in the sense that the people nodded and congratulated him on a fine piece of oratory. But where was God? Aren't many atheists grateful people? Didn't we know before we came to worship that gratitude is good? Yes, we forget. But were we ushered near to the very heart of God? Were we transformed as the Body of Christ, not merely as polite, pleasant citizens?

Listeners love conventional wisdom in the sermons they hear, and rank quite highly sermons that echo their favored sentiments. But if we mimic the best thoughts of the world, we do not point to Christ crucified. And if we provide an excuse for parroting notions that can be relished without God or the Body of Christ, we are no longer in the vicinity of the text that was a sermon before it was a text. So the sermon that works the way the text works will never, ever republish little catchy moralisms that could just have easily have been penned by Benjamin Franklin or Dear Abby.

Be very clear: many listeners, and even the powers that be, prefer sim-plistic, moralistic trivialities in the pulpit. Consider the dramatic sentence pronounced on an eloquent preacher in Alan Paton's *Cry the Beloved Country*: his voice "was of gold . . . as a deep bell when it is struck."

> The people sigh, and Kumalo sighs, as though this is a great word that has been spoken. And indeed this Msimangu is known as a preacher. It is good for the Government, they say in Johannesburg, that Msimangu preaches of a world not made by hands, for he touches people at the hearts, and sends them marching to heaven instead of to Pretoria. And there are white people who marvel. . . . Yet he is despised by some, for this golden voice that could raise a nation, speaks always thus. They say he preaches of a world not made by hands, while in the streets about him men suffer and strug-gle and die. They ask what folly is it that seizes upon so many of their people, making the hungry patient, the suffering content, the dying at peace? And how fools listen to him, silent, enrapt, sighing when he is done, feeding their empty bellies on his empty words.[3]

Would I be a "great preacher" sending people marching merely to heaven? Is the diet we serve nothing more than empty words? The ser-mon is not geared to please, and certainly not to please ourselves with the vain flattery of delighted listeners. We limp about in the shadows, stammering in hard places, naming the suffering, lingering in tears near the cross. Texts did not elicit sighs from those heading to heaven; but the heavenbound transformed their worlds—and ours!—by living into the texts that work this way and in no other.

WHAT ABOUT THE COMMENTARIES?

How do we avoid adding little catchy moralisms or jaded insertions of our own pet thoughts into the text? Here is where the commentaries, which have gone unmentioned so far, can help. I have never found a sermon in a commentary, although I was trained to look for sermons there. But scholarship plays a pivotal role; Robert Jenson has surmised that "the discovery and exploration of the oral and literary processes that eventuated in the Gospels beneficently *complicate* our involvement with the Gospel texts."[4]

The commentaries compel us to take the text seriously and to establish a nonnegotiable for every sermon: a clear sense among those listening that the text, and therefore the sermon, is anchored in the real world, in the historic course of human events. God spoke to Isaiah "in the year that King Uzziah died" (Isa. 6:1). Briefly, what then was the year 742 like in Jerusalem? David found Saul in a cave near the "Wildgoats' Rocks." (1 Sam. 24:2). Briefly, can you describe that terrain? Later, David saw Bathsheba bathing on her roof. Briefly, can you clarify that David's palace sat on the crest of a steep hill, all the houses of the city were perched on terraces below, and it was normal for bathing to happen on a roof (before the sermon launches into unrealities such as the notion that she was hoping to catch his eye)? Four men "dug" through the roof of a house in Capernaum to lower a sick man to Jesus (Mark 2:4). Briefly, can you mention that archaeologists have actually pinpointed this house, and why the word "dug" not only describes what the four would need to have done but also implies perhaps some dirt cascading down into the room on top of Jesus and whoever else was in there? Jesus asked his followers, "Who do people say that I am?" (Mark 8:27). Briefly, can you explain that they were not in a classroom with theological textbooks open, but outside, and standing in a city chock full of gaudy temples to various Roman deities? Paul and Silas sang hymns in jail at midnight (Acts 16:25). Briefly, can you paint a word picture of a first-century jail in a place like Philippi?

"Briefly" is the key. While some sermons never peek into the ancient world, others dwell at length back in Bible times, and the sermon never quite rises to the level of "sermon" and is little more than a Bible study talk. A Bible study talk is a good thing, but the sermon is not what God said (or did) once upon a time, but what God is saying today. Yet what God is saying today is profoundly rooted in what God said (or did) once upon a time. The preacher helps parishioners to see God's action in their real world if she portrays in tantalizing fashion the way God acted in the biblical world. A pilgrimage to the Holy Land can serve the preacher well; but with the availability of Internet photos of every archaeological site and geographical vista, every preacher can give the text a sense of place. Good commentaries can clarify social and political mores that factor into interpretation.

Facility in Hebrew and Greek is helpful—although I wonder about the proper deployment of what we may have mined from the ancient languages. If we announce (as I have many times) that the English translation just read is somewhat faulty and that the "real meaning" of the Greek is something rather different, might we unwittingly place handcuffs on readers, inducing the suspicious feeling that the words in the only Bible they might own are untrustworthy? Yet the explication of a given word can be beneficial, boring down into the depths of an idea that can become a significant embodiment of God's Word. In the prophets we read the word "justice." The preacher simply must introduce the full meaning of the Hebrew *mishpat*, which is not American-style justice (of the good being rewarded and the bad being punished), but the theologically marvelous insistence that the neediest be cared for. In the Gospels we hear a summons to "repent." The preacher must not fail the listeners, who suspect that repentance is some groveling, guilty mood, whereas *metanoia* is exceedingly hopeful in its true sense of "a change of mind."

A sermon can be quite "biblical" without simply parroting or repeating the Bible, and a preacher can cite a lot of Bible in a sermon but twist connotations and combine verses awkwardly in a way that distorts what is genuinely "biblical." C. S. Lewis, in his famous sermon on 2 Corinthians 4:17, "The Weight of Glory," declares,

> Indeed, if we consider the unblushing promises of reward and the staggering nature of the rewards promised in the Gospels, it would seem that Our Lord finds our desires not too strong, but too weak. We are half-hearted creatures, fooling about with drink and sex and ambition when infinite joy is offered us, like an ignorant child who wants to go on making mud pies in a slum because he cannot imagine what is meant by the offer of a holiday at the sea. We are far too easily pleased.[5]

Nowhere does the Bible say anything like "our desires are too weak," but Lewis has discerned quite shrewdly across a plethora of texts—and between the lines quite probingly—something imminently "biblical."

PERSONAL ATTENTION TO WORDS

How do we press beyond the superficial, flat-footed reading of a text? Later, we will explore the life of the preacher, and how we immerse ourselves in the delights and aches of the world. Granting a developed self, a more wide-eyed persona that is alert to the intersection of the world's dreams and wounds and the heart and activity of God in the world, we look at a text and wonder how it transformed anybody back then, and how it might transform anybody today. Some texts simply unveil the truth; they expose lies, and the preacher, like Dorothy's dog Toto, pulls back the curtain and simply reveals the truth people prefer not to hear, yet are also all too desperate to hear.

Think again about the story Jesus told about a man who tore down his barns to build bigger barns. How does that text work? Barn-builders are annoyed and want to say, "Yes, but big barns are better." But do bigger, better barns really matter? Not on the day that "your soul is required of you" (Luke 12:20). Actually, it's hard to preach on a text as simple and straightforward as this. Sometimes an economy of words can be more provocative, more poignant, than the compulsion to ramble for fifteen to twenty minutes. Simplicity, saying something well and briefly, may not only be memorable but actually capture more truth. Abraham Lincoln uttered America's greatest speech ever in a mere two minutes, using only 267 words; by the time the photographer was ready, Lincoln was turning to sit.

Close, deeply personal attention to the words, of course, is essential. The preacher may or may not know Greek or Hebrew, and probably if he does, our facility is embarrassingly slim. But digging into the original can make us more attentive, even if it only forces us to slow down, poke around not merely in a lexicon but in our souls, while dealing with even a single word. A superb training exercise might be to preach on the Psalms,[6] a bit of a lost art that served Augustine, Luther, and Calvin well enough. In the Psalms, we find images—as we do throughout the Bible, but nowhere as provocative as in the Psalms: a nesting stork, dogs growling, a rocky outcrop, a despised worm, the dew, smoke, a deer sniffing the air for a hint of water. Each image is like a still life. We take our watches off and examine the subtle hues, we listen for the breeze, we savor the wine's aftertaste.

Images appeal to the imagination. While the imagination can stray off onto silly homiletical tangents, Garrett Greene was right:

> Imagination turns out to be not the opposite of reality but rather the means by which manifold forms of both reality and illusion are mediated to us. Religions characteristically employ this power of imagination in order to make accessible the ultimate 'shape,' the organizing pattern, of reality itself, thereby illuminating the meaning and value of life.[7]

Our media culture almost requires that we "get" images, but I am not talking about playing to your audience because they dig Nike swooshes and little white apples on their portable technology. God works through signs; images are the way God delves into the soul. St.

Augustine suggested that God deploys signs "to conquer pride by work and to combat disdain in our minds, to which those things which are easily discovered seem frequently to become worthless."[8]

Could it be that the way texts work is by requiring work—not merely by the preacher but by the listeners? This isn't to slough blame off on them; but the wise preacher gives the congregation a few little jobs to do during the sermon, inviting them into the work of getting into an image or a sentence or a whole pericope. Work is required, and so is time.

Evidently, when Jesus preached, people didn't grasp what he said in a nanosecond. Their jaws dropped; they scratched their heads, stared at their sandals, and did lots of wondering. Texts take time to work, so the preacher must be patient, with a large strategy of not just this sermon but many over time. The preacher must leave time for people to think, reflect, ruminate during a single sermon; the working out of meaning might not happen until Tuesday—or a Tuesday in the year 2043. In *The Lord of the Rings*, J. R. R. Tolkien imagined talking trees, called Ents, who spoke an unusual language that perhaps suits the telling and hearing of the Gospel: "a lovely language, but it takes a very long time to say anything in it, because we do not say anything in it, unless it is worth taking a long time to say, and to listen to."[9]

Texts are portraits, not merely of God or Jesus or saints or martyrs. Texts paint me and you. They colorfully depict the nobility for which God made us; they expose the humiliating flaws that make us want to avert our gaze; and they paint who we could again be by the favor of God's mercy. Picasso once painted a portrait of Gertrude Stein. When he unveiled it (and it was, typically, a Picasso!), she allegedly responded, "But it doesn't look anything like me." He said, "Well, give it some time." Sermon strokes on the canvas of people's souls feel strange, hopeful, burdensome, offensive, delightful—and in time new creations happen right in front of you.

A WORD THAT CRIES OUT

Or we might peruse a text and circle a word or phrase that is intriguing—or more precisely, a word that cries out for attention, like the child in the classroom who sticks out, troubles the teacher, misbehaves—and it turns out that the child is acting out because the parents at home are at war with one another, or big sister is in the hospital battling leukemia. What is the moment in the text that cries out for help? or is pregnant with hidden life? Jesus told a story about a wealthy, pious man who inquired about salvation. What is the preacher to do? Focus on the perils of wealth?—which would be pleasing to poor or middle-class folk and mildly aggravating to wealthy parishioners. The man in the story claims to be righteous. Do we second-guess him and suggest he's a sinner in ways he can't self-diagnose?

Perhaps. But there is a word in the text that demands some attention, some tender care, some extended thought: "lack." "There is one thing you lack." Jesus is conversing with a guy who owns much and has plenty of religious activity too. But there is a "lack," something missing—and the sermon that works might probe this "lack" with people who also "lack" something. Of course, if you poll people to ask them what they "lack," they might name many shiny objects or personal wants. In fact, the list might grow, and frankly many people out there harbor a hidden disappointment with God because God has not supplied what they "lack."

Then we notice another word, without which "lack" appears to stump those of us prepared to craft a wish list to mail to Santa: "One." "One thing you still lack" (Luke 19:22). Gee, we lack many things, so could it be just "one"? How often in the stories of Jesus does this "one" come into play? Martha labors over many dishes, but Jesus upbraids her and suggests that "one thing is needful." A merchant sells everything he has to buy just "one" pearl. What is the "one" thing we "lack"? The preacher can explore this fruitfully.

But if Jesus is the speaker, if Jesus is the Gospel, then it might just be that the "one" thing is Jesus. The sermon might be tempted to say it is "faith" or "giving to the poor." But these "one" things are about us. The prickly child in the classroom might need a pencil or tutoring, but what the child really needs is a peaceful home or, quite simply, love. The sermon is about God, and the preacher points the sermon's bony finger to God: "Hear, O Israel, the LORD our God is one LORD" (Deut. 6:4), or as the Nicene Creed reminds us, "I believe in *one* God . . . and in *one* Lord Jesus Christ . . . of *one* substance with the Father."

I am always stunned by the way a single word, just spoken, lingering out there, can be laden with so much potential, its mere utterance flinging open windows into the soul. Just say the word "sadness," and someone will be pierced with pangs of sorrow; or mention that John Cheever once said the predominant mood of Americans in our day is "disappointment," and no one will wonder what you mean. The alluring words, like "joy" or "love" or "belonging," pique people's interest; and the sheer pronouncement of names—"Jesus" or "Jezebel" or "Mary" or "Judas"—evokes a swirl of emotions, a register of storied moments, possibilities, warnings, and invitations.

WORDS CHANGE MEANING

Words are the principal tools of the preacher's craft, and yet as preachers we tote around with us a peculiar lexicon. Perhaps the preacher's most daunting but lovely task is to expose the way words do not mean what they seem to mean, the care we use with words, the way we refill hollowed out words with newer, richer meaning. Writing about the Peloponnesian War, Thucydides spoke of a troubling epoch when, under the pressure of historical events, words changed their ordinary meanings.[10] Certainly, if God scandalously invaded the human realm, turned conventional wisdom on its head, and bolted from a heavily guarded tomb, then words can morph from the brown hard shell of common usage and emerge into colorful, delightful flight.

Not only does God publish a theological dictionary with definitions quite out of kilter with the culture's vapid jargon. We, those to whom God would speak, pervert words when we are fearful, or out of self-interest; there is a sinfulness in what we do with words. "Woe to those who call evil good and good evil, who put darkness for light and light for darkness, who put bitter for sweet and sweet for bitter!" (Isa. 5:20). Robert Lifton, reflecting on the way seemingly "good" Germans talked during World War II, spoke of "toxic euphemisms."[11] When the Nazis explained the violent atrocities of Kristallnacht, they said the events broke out "spontaneously"—not only a dodge of responsibility but also a slanderous indictment of the very population of Jews being set up. Words are thrown around with abandon, even manipulatively. Even when they are used with care, they may cloak theological problems.

Let us speak of freedom. No word outranks "freedom" in the lexicon of loaded words Americans love to say out loud. But biblical "freedom" is light years from our sense of being "free" to do what we want to do, to live in America, to make choices for ourselves with no authority looming over us. Augustine and Luther taught us that our allegedly free wills are shackled to sin. It is not that we are free to choose for or against God; we are bound, we are prisoners to self and the world until Christ in a liberating rescue of mercy sets us free. Even then, freedom isn't doing as I wish. Freedom is dependence, the lavish joy of being in yoked obedience to God. Freedom is not about me as an individual, but about being hitched to others in the Body of Christ.

Let us speak of justice. American-style justice is when the bad are punished and the good are rewarded. But the Old Testament features a marvelous Hebrew word translated "justice": *mishpat*, which is not fairness at all, but unfairness writ large in God's own hand. When you read the prophets, you find *mishpat* justice is when the poorest, the neediest, those left out by everybody else are cared for. A just society lifts up the lowly; an unjust society snidely urges them to lift themselves up by their own bootstraps.

Let us speak of love. Love is not that emotion that rushes or fails to rush. It is a commitment, a vision, getting in sync with the love of Christ. Let us speak of the meek, despised by the world as mousy, but lauded by Jesus as the ultimate inheritors of the earth. Let us speak of blessedness. How crass of Bruce Wilkinson in his bestselling *The Prayer of Jabez* to feed into American consumerism and greed by suggesting that God has warehouses of stuff boxed up for us, "blessings"—if only we back up the SUV and pick them up! Jesus said the "blessed" were the poor, or those "persecuted for righteousness' sake" (Matt 5:10).

Words matter, and the loving, subtle art of redefinition requires considerable dexterity and uncommon wisdom. If we get the words wrong, if we feed into people's preexisting craving for freedom, justice, love, and blessing as debased in the world's misconstrual of the good life, than we would do better simply to sit and not rise into a pulpit until we get our vocabulary straight. The words do work, though, since God not only created words but created everything that is, simply by speaking. "In the beginning was the Word, the Word was with God. . . . all things were made through the Word" (John 1:1, 3).

MOVEMENT IN THE TEXT

Back to the Psalter: some Psalms "work" by way of an evocative image. Others "work" by movement. Something is going on in this Psalm, something shifts, a drama is unfolding. Scholars have long believed that many Psalms originated in a sanctuary, where a worshiper cries out in desperation, and the priest replies with some word of hope. Hannah pours out her soul in Shiloh, and Eli blesses her (1 Sam. 1:17). The one who prays is transported to a new psychic zone. Every Psalm turns from despair to hope. Let us hear what Spurgeon preached on Psalm 13:

> What a change is here! Lo, the rain is over and gone, and the time of the singing of birds is come. The mercy seat has so refreshed the poor weeper, that he clears his throat for a song. If we have mourned with him, let us now dance with him. David's heart was more often out of tune than his harp. He begins many of his Psalms sighing, and ends them singing.[12]

Isn't the heart of the Gospel this movement from sin to forgiveness, from cross to resurrection, from isolation to community?

Notice physical movement in texts. Jesus confronts the rich young ruler, and he turns his body and walks away. How swiftly does he spin away? Soldiers seize Jesus; how forcefully? The father runs to welcome the prodigal son. Peter moves from a dim understanding of Jesus to a truer discipleship. Paul preaches, and a crowd surges. Too often we imagine Jesus sitting still; we think of most texts and biblical talkers as potted plants in some still-life painting. I love the Pasolini film *The Gospel according to St. Matthew*. Here Jesus strides forcefully, is on the move, in a hurry, talking over his shoulder to his disciples, who breathlessly try to keep up. Texts exhibit movement, physical and theological, and sermons move in time with the movement of the text.

The most important movement in our texts, the most essential responsibility of every sermon, is hauling the lone seeker out of loneliness toward the heart of God and into faithful community. The way texts work is to move people out of a solo existence into the Body of Christ, rescuing them from a thicket of addictive relationships and into the freedom of mutual dependence in the Church. Our next chapter will pay close attention to the "ranking of subjects," which not only recommends a way to stay faithfully focused on the castle and its contents, but also can get us out of quite a few jams.

For now we mention a few other issues to consider when we ask, how do texts work? Texts work in some room or another. Consider the feel of the pew or chairs on which people sit, the way the light filters through stained glass or shines out of spotlights, the crafting of the woodwork or an image on a screen, the temperature and humidity. Jesus stood up in a synagogue in Nazareth (Luke 4:16). On the day of Pentecost they were sitting in a house when the Spirit rushed (Acts 2:2). When the forlorn disciples were in a room, Jesus suddenly appeared to them (John 20:19). Moses walked into the court of Pharaoh. Isaiah was virtually annihilated before the cherubim in the temple. Jesus was in a house when somebody bored through the roof and lowered an invalid. A woman approached Jesus at table and poured a flask of oil on him. Does the room where you preach work with this text, compete against the text, heighten its impact, rob it of its depth?

How do texts work? They work in worship: What has been sung? What is about to be sung, or prayed, or announced? A text happens in a season: we read ominous words Jesus uttered the night before he died—but we hear them in the lectionary well into the season of Easter! "The Word became flesh" is one thing in December, quite another in July. A text works in a culture, in a town, in a neighborhood where something happened just yesterday. We will think more later about the world in which we find ourselves, but for the moment it is worth noting that a text is read, heard, and expounded in a tangible context, a building with people in a mood. The preacher can learn to pick up on cues, reverberations off the walls, emotions dragged in the door, all of which have an often unnoticed but weighty impact on the way a text works. While we are not always able to anticipate these last-second adaptations that may be required of us, we can be solid in preparation in determining what we'll talk about, and what we won't talk about, and in proper order.

4

Ranking the Subjects

In the *Euthyphro*, Plato imagines a charioteer driving two horses. One soars upward toward the heavens, nobly, but battles against the other, who darkly tugs the reins toward what is lowly; the chariot driver can hardly keep them together and in check. Preachers, almost every week, find themselves steering between competing urges. One is the lofty aim of theological wisdom, saying something exegetically sound and doctrinally faithful. The other, which wins out too often, is the very pragmatic need to get something on paper, to find an angle, something that will work and be preachable enough come Sunday. And, of course, we battle the constant tension between striving to be faithful pastors and preachers and the competing demands of trying to be faithful to family, housework, and oneself by getting a little rest now and then.

We suspect that these two horses of truth and practicality need not be so hard to steer. When younger preachers ask me about this, my most helpful hint, my most cunning way out of the inevitable stuckness that plagues me when I am trying to find something to say, is simultaneously the best theological wisdom I can muster, really the most profound lesson from the great cloud of witnesses who have filled pulpits for two millennia now. When I am struggling with a text, flailing with too many unpromising ideas on the computer screen, wondering if I am blasting people for being too impious or letting them off too easily for being spiritually sweet, scratching my head at my failure to diagnose the human condition properly, agonizing over what the sermon's result ought to be, I often step back and remember: It's about God.

IT'S NOT ABOUT YOU

I recall a prickly moment on a family vacation when our kids were little. Somebody said something or another, a moment turned sour, I felt wounded and put on my best pouty face. And my wife, in her frustration, eyed me and declared, "Not everything is about you!" Ouch! That made me feel worse. But she was right, and I've remembered her verbal remonstrance many times when I have found myself on the verge of feeling disregarded, boxed out, or emotionally shoved. It's not always about me.

Sermons aren't always about us. Karl Barth wrote that to speak of God is *not* to speak of humanity in a loud voice.[1] Be very clear: the majority of sermons preached aren't about God, but about us. The bestselling authors, the most popular television preachers, and many megachurch orators do not speak much about God, but about us. What was the title of Joel Osteen's bestseller? *Become a Better You: Seven Keys to Improving Your Life Every Day*. Catchy, appealing—but not everything is about you. The sermon's subject is God. In fact, if there is some elusive "better you" to be achieved, it will come only when we stop focusing on "you" (from the preacher's point of view, "me" from the listener's), when our narcissism is broken, when we discover ourselves to be "lost in wonder, love, and praise." The sermon peers into God's castle, not at our own navels.

Too often we fret over what people want to hear, or what their "needs" might be, or even what the needs or inner psyche of ancient people might have been and how Jesus dealt with such things. Spiritually, people are tangled in confusion about desire, and "felt needs" become a golden idol before whom not only people out there, but even the preachers, bow in humble adoration. We could provide correction on notions of need, along the lines of C. S. Lewis (who preached a fantastic sermon[2] declaring that our desires are not too strong, but too weak!). Even salvation itself too easily becomes yet another commodity, and the preacher risks centering the sermon on the people instead of upon God in the very proclamation of the crucifixion! Sam Wells has diagnosed the sneaky trouble: "The day of salvation is no longer the day Christ died or the day he rose from the grave but is now the day I was born again. The story is no longer fundamentally about God: God is now a character in a story that is fundamentally about me."[3]

What if the sermon is about God? What if the stated purpose of the sermon isn't to resolve any inner human problem, or to stir up some feeling, or even to incite people to action, but quite simply to say true things about God, to glorify God, and the sermon's only real outcome is a mood of praise? I have always struggled with the transfiguration; every sermon has felt half baked, because I am wondering how the three disciples felt, why they went down the mountain, how my listeners should think about the Old and New Testaments or retreating from pious moments into a world of action. But the first disciples, who "saw" the "sermon," who witnessed the event, were nothing but dumbfounded: "They fell on their faces, and were filled with awe" (Matt. 17:6).

Think about the temptation narrative. Three times the Devil tempted Jesus, and the predictable sermon (about us!) begins: "We are tempted. How do we resist temptation?" But perhaps the text isn't about us at all! It was Jesus who survived a headlong assault from Satan himself. I would wither, eat the rocks I just transmuted into bread, and seize power over the kingdoms after leaping into the arms of angels. Perhaps the text is about the greatness of Jesus. Thank God Jesus was Jesus, that he didn't succumb, that my salvation resides not in my lame imitations of him, but rather in his stalwart defeat of evil. A sermon then can relax in a way. We can wad up the paper on which we were jotting notes on how people are seized with urges to leap from tall buildings, and devise a sermon that is little more than a paean of praise, a hymn of glorification.

Virtually every sermon can benefit from this simple shift of focus. The wheat and the tares: I heard several preachers last lectionary cycle get ensnared in curious psychological analyses of whether we are wheat, or tares, or both wheat and tares, or sometimes wheat and sometimes tares. But just perhaps, Jesus is talking about God! God is the kind of God who can bear wheat and tares. The preacher need squander no time—and more importantly no preparation time and energy—probing the inner selves of listeners. To look into the heart of such a God, though, liberates the sermon to glorify a God for whom we can quite reflexively be grateful.

SOLVING PROBLEMS

The heart of every sermon is about God, not you or me. Obviously this truth carries an implicit criticism of the sort of preaching most of us were reared on, the homiletical tradition whose godfather was probably Harry Emerson Fosdick, who declared that *every* sermon "should have for its main business the solving of some problem—a vital, important problem, puzzling minds, burdening consciences, distracting lives."[4] A sermon that is "about" anything other than God risks placing me, my problems, my needs, my life as the true center of the universe—as if it might be that were I to have a happier marriage, or a better job, or less anxiety, then God's kingdom would have dawned. My marriage and job and anxiety are not trivial really, but the sermon should usher us into something far larger, more magnificent.

I have no doubt that a well-conceived sermon on a text, with God as the primal subject, will inevitably solve quite a few problems—and certainly raise a few new problems! The Gospel isn't the resolution to my difficulties—as the martyrs could well teach us—but at times becomes the conveyer of a whole new set of problems we never imagined before we subjected ourselves to a sermon. People do have problems, feelings in need of healing, lackluster marriages that could improve, habits requiring conversion. The paradox is that when we see God, we are swept up into a mood of praise; we relativize and even cure what felt like a problem five minutes before we turned our focused gaze upon God. Bonhoeffer, writing from prison, was on target when he said that repentance is "not in the first place thinking about one's own needs, problems, sins, and fears, but allowing oneself to be caught up into the way of Jesus Christ."[5]

The grave risk—and no one in any pew will ever recognize the peril or ask for our assistance—is what worried St. Augustine, as summarized by Jason Byassee: "Part of our problem as creatures is that we overestimate the importance of the glimpses of earthly beauty we can see and mistake these for all the beauty there is, when they are meant to lead us to the true beauty of God, whose beauty is veiled in the form of Christ's ugliness."[6]

A sermon could be entirely about God—much of the Bible is; in fact most of the Psalms are. A sermon could simply take fifteen minutes to extol the grandeur of God or to plumb the wonders of God's wisdom; a sermon could be nothing more than an admiration of the beauty of Jesus Christ, God's holy Son, his beautiful body, his immense compassion, his intimacy with the Father, his impatience with self-righteousness, his wondrous love, the sacred head now wounded, sorrow and love flow mingled down. Why should the choir and the hymn singers greedily seize all the fun of praise during a service? What purer homiletical offering might the preacher make? The Word did become flesh, and we will spend a chapter on how to make earthy, believable connections and applications between the Word and our life in the flesh; nothing is gained by preaching a dry theological treatise. But the sermon must be essentially about God, focused on the wonder and glory of God.

If the sermon spoke eloquently about God, or even feebly to God, might Fosdick's entire equation about problems and needs be turned inside out? Speaking to God on the printed page, Hans Urs von Balthasar perhaps set a tone for a kind of preaching that is attentive first and always to God's Spirit:

> We always wanted to measure your fulfillments by the standard of our desires. More than what our hollow space contains, so we thought, we cannot obtain from you. But when your Spirit began to blow in us, we experienced so much greater space that our own standard became meaningless to us. We noticed the first installment and pledge of a wholly other freedom. . . . And thus is fulfilled the promise which is the blowing Spirit itself in person: Because he blows the fulfillment toward us. He does it infallibly, if we are ready to allow ourselves to be surpassed in our desires. The religion and desire of all peoples means ultimately this: to get beyond one's own desires.[7]

Even in sermons where we want to lead people to be good, or to serve the poor, or to give more money, or to shed prejudice, or whatever, we need to get straight to the God sections. Sermons get stuck in "Paul said this to the Corinthians," or "Isaiah said these things to the Israelites," and never, or very haltingly, get to "God is saying this to us today." What was Jesus' offense in Nazareth that made them want to throw him off a cliff? He stood in the synagogue, read what Isaiah said to the Israelites back then, closed the scroll, and said, "Today this Scripture has been fulfilled" (Luke 4:21). Karl Barth's goal in his scintillating commentary on Romans is what we are after: "to wrestle with [the text], till the walls which separate" our current century from the first "become transparent . . . until a distinction between yesterday and today becomes impossible."[8] Too daring? Are we too timid to speak for God? Do we (rightly) tremble over the prospect of getting it wrong, or attaching God to my pet notions? We had better be scared! But we had best throw caution to the wind and leap boldly. Will Willimon was right: what Barth admired about preachers quite simply is that "they dare."[9]

THE SECOND SUBJECT

Of course, the preacher cannot talk only about God—although the risk would be well worth taking. Jesus spoke of people, their lives, their wounds, their faith, their future. How do we speak not just of God but of "you"? The title of this chapter is "Ranking the Subjects." The number one subject of a sermon can and should be God. But is number two me, or you? There is a middle subject, in our rankings a fair distance ahead of you/me/the individual listener. It's "you," but English fails us, as other languages do not, so let us resort to Southern English: after God as top-ranked subject, number two is "y'all." Many sermon quandaries can be resolved if we remember we are speaking to and about the Body of Christ, the corporate community out there.

Too many sermons feel as if I am in the pulpit speaking into a tin can, and my can has lots of little strings draped across the sanctuary, each string attached to a little can that each listener holds to his or her ear. Yes, there are quite a few people in the room, but the sermon is a one-to-one, preacher-to-individual listener experience. But the sermon is to the Body, to the Church, and its goal is to move the Church, not to move persons individually, perhaps the way movie producers imagine appealing to a single moviegoer. We preach to the Body.

Quite a few Christians have told me that their favorite Bible verse is Jeremiah 29:11: "I know the plans I have for you, says the LORD, plans for welfare and not for evil, to give you a future and a hope." God has "a plan for my life"—or so they profess to me. As appealing as this may be, and as caring and personal as God always is, the fact is the Bible doesn't say a word about God having a blueprint, a script, a "plan" for *my* life, how *I* will grow up, whom *I* will marry, how things will unfold, even when I will die. In a way, such a "plan" might be comforting; but then do we really want to be pawns on God's chessboard? Is God devising some misery for you next week?

If we read Jeremiah 29:11 carefully, we notice that God's "plans for good" are not for Jeremiah or any other individual. The word "you" (in "the plans I have for you") is plural; in the South, God would say "the plans I have for *y'all.*" The future, the hope God gives "you" ("y'all"), is for a crowd, for the community, for the nation. God called Jeremiah to speak God's Word, not to this man or woman, or to you or me, but to the nation of Israel during its most perilous time in history. The text works by declaring to the Body that God has plans for y'all. We do our listeners the greatest favor by gifting them with a place in that community, the dizzying privilege of being part of something bigger than just *me* or *my life,* a far better destiny than some mere solo adventure with the Divine.

So how can ranking God number one and Church number two help a sermon? Suppose our text is Mark 4:3–9. Most sermons think of the parable and ask, "What kind of soil am I? Am I thorny or rocky? Am I fertile soil in which God's Gospel seeds can grow?" But what if the sermon is about God, which is likely what Jesus intended? What kind of crazy sower is this, flinging seed all over the place, even in spots where nobody else would waste a single seed? This profligate sower, this spendthrift farmer, seems happy to waste the seed, to be sure it gets spread all around. Clearly God is like this, for we have never seen any sort of human sower who would bother tossing it on the road.

After God, the sermon is about the Church. The question is then, "What kind of sower are *we* as a church?" If we are close to the heart of God, if we intend to be the Body of Christ on earth, the literal hands and feet of Christ on this planet, then perhaps we fling, we do not measure parsimoniously. We are not forever careful, fearful of failure—but we fling it with abandon. We try crazy possibilities happily, not much bothered by seed that some bird scoops up, not shackled by budget worries, but delighting only in ensuring that the Church gets the love spread all over the place.

IT'S ABOUT THE BODY

The lectionary presented me with Philippians 4:1–9 the Sunday after a horrific stock-market crash that particularly clubbed a large bank in my city. I knew I would be preaching to anxious, fearful, sad, angry people. At first, Paul's admonition "Do not be anxious" felt like a gift straight from heaven, and I began to craft one of those tin-can walkie-talkie sermons to each individual: "Hey, you, the guy on row seven in the blue jacket: Don't be anxious!" But I recalled my own rules: it's about God, and it's about the Church.

A far better sermon resulted. People, I predicted correctly, may have felt anxious about their jobs or homes, but when they came to church, they were literally wondering what would happen to the church. Is there an anxious church? Indeed—and the sermon had to address the role of the church in tough times, this "shelter from the stormy blast," and how the Church "is of God and will be preserved to the end of time," the enduring, unshakable existence of this place where we come as individuals for hope, but also where we find love and community, the true antidotes to anxiety.

But how is "Do not be anxious" about God? We can't oversimplify and say, "If you just trust God, you won't be anxious." That would be a lie. It's about God: God is not anxious. Banks can fail; economies may crumble; but God is not anxious. God is the ultimate nonanxious presence. In fact, Paul wrote these words during atrocious economic times, at the end of his life, chained to a Roman soldier, with Rome in conflagration all around him. Was Paul anxious? Probably not any more than when he had been in a Philippian jail years earlier. Was Paul a psychic wonder to be able to sing and be joyful in horrible moments? I don't think so. His mind was on God; his sermon, like his life, was about God. When Paul said, "If there is any excellence, if there is anything worthy of praise" (Phil. 4:8), he wasn't reminding us to count our blessings or to think positively. He was on the brink of death, chained and bowed down, but looking up into heaven, anticipating his imminent togetherness with Jesus. "Is there anything worthy of praise?" Are you kidding? We have Jesus. Anything excellent? Think on these things. Preach on these things.

Years ago I circled a profound thought in a book I cannot find any longer: "The antidote to despair is praise." I would add "and community." Yes, get around to preaching on the individual. But maybe you don't really need to, because if your sermons are praise, if they are about God, if they are about the Body, if they draw us together toward God, then the individuals in front of you don't seem like isolated solo spiritual practitioners, but members, not on a roll, but in the Body, really just one, their anxiety mysteriously diminished as they are together lost in wonder, love, and praise, as they love and are loved in the fellowship of the saints.

Stepping back, once sermon preparation has begun, especially once it has bogged down, and asking whether the sermon is about God or about the Body, is not merely a helpful strategy to get the sermon finished. What we are after is the beautiful song of what genuinely is the

Gospel. We want what has been taught and handed down through the ages. We want truth. But before we explore How to Tell the Truth, let me share this addendum on ranking the subjects for preaching. We always have a handful of parishioners who do not mind jamming sermon ideas into the suggestion box. No one has ever said, "Here is a biblical text I wish you would preach on," but many have topics, subjects, themes about which they think they would like to hear some homiletical wisdom: marriage, friendship, the decay of morals, why bad things happen. Of course, we reply with immense patience and love, and try valiantly to clarify that we preach on texts, not topics. Perhaps the suggested topics are burning questions that should in fact be addressed in a sermon, but only after we have first been attentive to where a text might lead to connections between these people who have sermon suggestions and God (and each other).

JULY 4 AND MOTHER'S DAY

The greatest hazard comes when the suggested topics are problematical theologically or they cloak a not-so-subtle criticism of or sad disappointment in you as pastor. Two dates on the calendar pose peculiar challenges: Mother's Day and July 4. On the Sunday that looms nearest July 4 (or Memorial Day or Veterans' Day), many American Christians yearn for something "patriotic," whether this means singing "God Bless America," a message on the sacrifices soldiers have made for our freedom or the wisdom of the Founding Fathers, or perhaps saying the pledge of allegiance. How we cope with these requests (which may be subtle and sweet or shrill and angry) might range from simply ignoring the national day in question, or knuckling under and just letting them have their way, or even waging theological combat against patriotic usurpations of Christianity.

But why do people care so much and feel so passionately about these matters? We can diagnose various flaws in theological formation or in the civic religion that dominates our culture. At the end of the day, people (like people in other nations!) have a kind of fealty to America, a pride in their homeland, a deep desire for God to be meaningfully connected to their nation, their society. The impulse can be lovely, and there must be ways to tap into the more promising side of that impulse without feeding the dark side. I too often have not reckoned thoroughly enough with the fact that I seem unsufficiently patriotic to

Church members for whom military and patriotic matters are viscerally powerful. I have preached against wars, against armaments, against an America-first mood, against patriotic arrogance, without a robust pastoral awareness in myself that I am talking in front of people who got off carriers and stormed a beach at Normandy and saw friends left and right shot dead, people who sent sons off to the insane jungles of Vietnam and saw them return home mangled, people who served nobly and with little remuneration in the armed forces, people whose sense of self has been shaped by family and heroes who value what I seem to be trouncing.

Aren't there ways to acknowledge what they hold dear without a triumphal acclamation of all Americana, without endorsing a war or political party, without perverting the Gospel's understanding of words like "freedom," yet also without appearing to be ignorant or unappreciative or just plain insensitive? Surely, while treating the text of the day, we can forage about and find some illustration from American history that might faithfully embody what we are trying to say.

George Washington did not leave his soldiers alone at Valley Forge but suffered every discomfort they did. Perhaps the incarnation of God's Word is like that. Once near Memorial Day my text led me into an exploration of why bad things happen, and I reflected on the memories a friend shared from his experience on Omaha Beach in 1944. Another July 4, I thumbed through the remarkable correspondence between Thomas Jefferson and John Adams, two longtime enemies who mellowed and became cherished friends before dying on July 4, 1826, exactly fifty years after the signing of the Declaration of Independence. People who adore July 4 felt entirely enfranchised, but I said not one word about the grandeur of America or that God birthed this country for some manifest destiny, but instead spoke of the reconciliation of enemies.

Mother's Day, which always falls on a Sunday, and to a far lesser extent in our culture, Father's Day, pose intriguing challenges. People may come to Church with mother, worship being the fulcrum of a special day, and failure to mention Mother's Day or "the many wonderful things our mothers have done for us" will strike worshipers as simply inexplicable, even offensive. In my parishes, I have always had members press me to honor the oldest mother, or the mother with the most children, or the mother with the newest child, or mothers period (with little gifts, like a carnation handed to each mother when entering the sanctuary). These gestures can and must be handled graciously but firmly. Do we refuse a carnation to the woman battling infertility, or to the woman whose only child died last year and barely was able to muster the courage to show up in worship? Perhaps a mother (or father) was abusive, or simply icy, and daffy talk of how nifty moms are can plunge a knife into the very people who need us the most on a day like Mother's (or Father's) Day.

Again, to ignore the moment is to miss an opportunity to bring people closer to their Church family, both for those who are giddy and hugging their mom, but also for those who are grieving the mother they lost or perhaps never really had in the first place. There are ways to preach the text of the day, and yet to find something to say about a mother, somebody's mother, or even the way the Bible thinks of God in maternal images, which can be a healing salve to the wounded. If motherhood must be mentioned in some way, why not think about our ranking of the subjects, and go first to Mary, the mother of our Lord? Why not, on Mother's Day, speak tenderly of the remarkable love she had for Jesus, how she heard the stunning angel's commission, how she battled the shame to seek Joseph's understanding; how she felt the first stirrings in her belly; how she must have cried out during delivery, only to welcome Jesus' first cry; how she held him, nursed him, counted his fingers, watched him take his first steps, heard his first words, took pride in his maturation but then learned to fear for his very life, and finally watched as the lifeblood she had given him drained out of his pure, holy body—and as even in that moment he asked the Beloved Disciple to take care of her?

If God is our first subject and the Church is the second, what better day than Mother's Day to invite the Church to be the Mother, to look to our children and love them, teach and nurture them—and not only our own children but perhaps with more zeal those who have no mothers, the homeless, the destitute?

There is a lovely, if confused, truth hidden in our society's celebrations of those special days that people wish we would attend to more frothily. As we notice that kernel of truth, we adhere gingerly to the larger truth we are commissioned to preach, and to the Body we are commissioned to pastor. So it is this larger truth that will require our attention now.

Where Sermons Happen

5

How to Tell the Truth

Once upon a time, Karl Barth suggested that the question people consider as the sermon unfolds is simple: "Is it true?" As we will see, that is at best only one of many questions they lug into the sanctuary with them, one that may be outweighed by what seem to be more measly concerns (like "Is he a good speaker?" "Do I agree with her politics?" "When is this over? "What's for lunch?"). But surely we would demand of ourselves, as an undebatable baseline, that we want to say true things, or to do something even grander: to tell "the truth."

To speak truly, there are quite a few "of course" items on every preacher's checklist. Of course, the sermon must be exegetically sound. Of course, the sermon must be sufficiently interesting to keep people from drifting off to sleep. Of course, the local context must be taken into account—or we should say, contexts must be taken into account: the larger cultural context in which we all operate, but also the quite specific, peculiar, very local context. The preacher must grow multiple sensors, barometers, weather vanes, speedometers, whatever it takes to be attuned to the people and what they can bear, when to push, when to chill or be tender. Of course you have to know the people and their hurts, dreams, lunacies, and charm. Solid, attentive engagement in pastoral care and simply sharing in the life of the community are essentials for the preaching task. We are attentive to people and to the culture, but we never merely mirror the base reality we notice back to people, or let what we detect bend what should be the Gospel.

A sermon, the best conceivable sermon, should rise to the following standard: this sermon works only here, today, in this place with
these people, not last year with these people or next year, and not
with some other people, or in another room. The sin of plagiarism is
not theft; it is gross insensitivity, thinking a sermon written for some
other people in some other place and some other time could work in
this place and this time with these people. Find the timely word, and
don't even keep your old sermons, because they are quickly as dull as
yesteryear's fashion.

Yet, as correct as what I just wrote has always seemed to me, I think
about something I read from the pen of Phillips Brooks, the great Civil
War–era preacher who wrote "O Little Town of Bethlehem." After
encouraging pastors to know their congregations, Brooks added that a
preacher needs regularly to preach to people he does not know,

> to keep the truth which he preaches as large as it ought to be. He
> who ministers to the same people always, knowing them minutely,
> is apt to let his preaching grow minute, to forget the world, and
> to make the same mistakes about the gospel that one would make
> about the force of gravitation if he came to consider it a special
> arrangement made for these few operations which it accomplishes
> within his house.[1]

Famous for the image of the Bible in one hand and the newspaper in the other, Karl Barth warned his preaching students against the
presumed need that every sermon must be as timely as this morning's
newspaper. "We do not always have to bring in the latest and most sen-
sational events." Events belong to everyday life, "but now it is Sunday,
and people do not want to remain stuck in everyday problems. They
want to go beyond them and rise above them." He reminisced over the
way he preached on the Sunday after the sinking of the *Titanic* and
made the disaster the main theme of the sermon. The result? "A mon-
ster of a full-scale *Titanic* sermon." When war broke out in 1914, he
raged in all his sermons about the war, until a woman came and begged
him to talk about something else. "She was right! I had disgracefully
forgotten the importance of submission to the text. All honor to relevance, but pastors should be good marksmen who aim their guns
beyond the hill of relevance."[2]

So, although I always feel awkward preaching out on the road, as
if I am talking through thick glass to people getting muffled impres-
sions of what I'm trying to say, and although I do believe the best

sermon is the one that works today, in this place, and with these people, I see the pitfalls of "relevance" and the imperative to aim higher. Probably the preacher, when preparing a sermon, must cling tightly to both the timeliness of this sermon this week to these people and the bigger, broader "this is God's Word always, anywhere, to anybody" undertone.

This is what the apostle Paul achieved in his letters. When he wrote the Galatians, he quite pointedly addressed what was going on there, and then, something quite different from what was going on in Corinth, much less to a single individual with an issue, Philemon. Yet there is a "coherence"[3] of thought, a single melody being applied with one tonality in Thessalonica, yet with a slightly different rhythm and harmonization in Philippi, as Paul instinctively grasped the contingencies in each congregation and city. The very timeliness of Paul's message unveils an essential aspect of the Gospel and the requirement of preaching: God acted in Christ once upon a time, but the Word and action of the Spirit create a living, pulsating, startlingly personal encounter now, and we preach best when we mimic the fashion of Paul talking at the intersection of timeless and timely.

CLARITY OF MOVES

Truth in preaching can be wasted by simple failure to speak or think clearly. I hear preachers tied up in knots, obviously with quite profound things to say, but clueless as to how to get it out of their mouths. Many preaching books suggest how sermons should be constructed to achieve clarity, and I don't have much to add. David Buttrick's instruction regarding "moves" has always proven beneficial to me and those I teach and mentor: a "move" is a "formed module," a little section of your talk that is discrete, perhaps memorable, and you pause before moving to the next "move." Some sermons, unfortunately, are like a garden hose, water spewing forth continuously, but listeners can't follow the stream for so long and wind up feeling . . . hosed.

Some sermons indeed have discrete moves, but sadly just too many of them. This is hard: you come up with a good "move." I'll tell them about the incident at the homeless shelter, or I'll explicate the meaning of the Greek word *aletheia*, or it might be interesting to pass along this juicy quotation from Frederick Buechner. All good moves—and you hate to keep a good move to yourself! But a sermon with eight or eleven or thirteen moves befuddles the listener. Five or six moves generally will do, which means you may have to jettison a lovely idea—or invest it in the bank for another day, another sermon. Most sermons I hear, including my own, try to do too much, and dump too much on the poor listener, who does not enjoy the benefit of seeing your manuscript or having sat with you throughout the agonizing preparation process.

Once you settle on the five or six moves, the daunting challenge becomes structure or order, and all I can recommend is experimentation. With word processing, it's easy to shuffle. You have five moves or clumps of things you wish to say: A, B, C, D and E. Is the best order the one that by happenstance landed in your notes, ABCDE? What would ABDEC be like? Let's try BCDEA! What is the emotional flow? Which order has the craftier impact? What is a lovely idea that could best be tossed? Perhaps instead of BCDEA we give them only BCEA, or CDEA, or even BDE. I preach five times on a Sunday morning, and even in the course of the morning I learn what you might need to figure out on Saturday if you preach only once: BCEA works far better than ABCDE, and it may even be that idea D is the wittiest, wisest of all my ideas. But on this day, with this message to these people, D is a distraction, a catchy one that actually seduces everybody away from the Gospel logic of BCEA.

There is no flawless solution, and we always toddle and bump our heads. When I am about to throw up my hands in exasperation with this structural nightmare, I recall the marvelous commiseration and insight of Annie Dillard, who spoke of writing books but could just as well have been talking to you and me about sermon preparation:

> Every book has an intrinsic impossibility, which its writer discovers as soon as his first excitement dwindles. The problem is structural; it is insoluble. Complex stories have this problem—the prohibitive structural defect the writer wishes he had never noticed. He writes in spite of that. He finds ways to minimize the difficulty; he strengthens other virtues; he cantilevers the whole narrative out into thin air, and it holds.[4]

Sunday dawns, and you go with BCEA and leave the cantilevering to God. Never forget, on Tuesday or Thursday or even Saturday night, that in order to tell the truth, you have to keep it simple. Clarity is everything.

THE GRAVEST PERIL

Well, not quite everything. The most important book of recent years that I would say every preacher (if not every person) simply must read has the rather impolite title of *On Bullshit*.[5] The author, a professor of moral philosophy at Princeton University named Harry Frankfurt, isn't trying to be cheeky; rather, he has quite brilliantly diagnosed and analyzed the pervasive mood of communication in our culture. The essence of BS is not that the BSer says things that are untrue. The BSer, in fact, is utterly uninterested in what is true or false. BS is the calculating art of trying to get away with something not entirely noble. The BSer is trying to talk you into something and will say anything to get you to do what the BSer wants. BS is phony talk, designed not to reveal truth or honor the listener, but only to work and serve the self-absorbed intentions of the BSer. BS is rampant, and we have come to accept it as normal. Politicians, advertisers, business colleagues, car salespersons: we think we are wise to BS, but its prevalence numbs our attentiveness to the mere possibility of truth.

To speak of "truth" itself feels like BS. Somebody has their "truth," and they attach God or reason to their truth and demand you give assent. So the very theologically necessary notion of truth raises suspicions—rightly!—in our day and age. The cloud that hangs over every pulpit involves BS. People suspect the sermon may just be more BS. To reveal what is good or true, the preacher must acknowledge the vapid expectation of BS out there, strive gallantly for clarity, and pray for truth to poke its way through the pile.

The BS complication in preaching is more complicated than we think. The preacher, no less than the car salesman or the politician, has grown accustomed to BS and may not know how else to talk or think. The preacher has stuff he must get done, objectives she is hoping to achieve, and the sermon feels like the best chance to accomplish something. So say anything, talk them into that mission trip, or giving more money, or joining the Church. Our ability to perceive and pass on truth is jeopardized and compromised by the BS that has wedged its way into our own souls. What is the preacher to do? Be wary, very wary, and doggedly vigilant of BS. Find a trusted friend who will detect and name the BS in your talk. Avoid even the slightest hint of "I'll say this to get them to . . ." in homiletical preparation.

At one level BS is a problem, but BS is so pervasive and so much beloved in our culture because . . . well, because people have BS receptors in their souls. We may feel annoyed by all the BS out there. Yet BS seems to work—but why? Not only does the BSer say whatever he needs to say to dupe the BSee into doing whatever; the BSee is not all that fond of truth, the BSee wishes to be flattered, to be told exactly what they want to hear. People love BS in the sermons they hear. Give them what they expect, what soothes their egos; avoid what might trample on their sensitivities—and they will love you and rank you as a great master of the pulpit.

So how do we preach when BS is the very air we breathe in the sanctuary? Simple cognizance of the terrifying possibility of BS keeps us on guard. Ask somebody who's listening: any BS here? Talk about BS in the sermon itself, to equip people with the BS detectors that they need, not only out there when they are peppered with advertising or office chatter, but also when listening to you! Admit you need to talk people into certain things, and do it over coffee instead of over the top of the pulpit. Find and pursue diligently the uncomfortable edge in every text, not the one people don't want to hear, but the one you frankly would prefer not to preach. Secure a preaching mentor who will listen to your sermons—or watch them (as some BS is in facial expression and gesture!)—and then be so kind as to tell you lovingly "I feel the BS piling up over there."

SLEEPING WITH EXTRATERRESTRIALS

Be very sure: people walk in with plenty of BS in their minds. Worshipers, to a person, walk in the door with some theology. We never preach to a blank slate, but to minds that have been scribbled on all week. People bring with them all kinds of spiritualities they have picked up at work, from TV, on the Internet, off the bookshelves. We are wrong to suppose that people either are some brand of Christian, or not religious at all. Wendy Kaminer's book *Sleeping with Extra-Terrestrials: The Rise of Irrationalism and Perils of Piety* should be required reading for every preacher. She demonstrates how Americans are very, very spiritual indeed, indulging in an extravagant smorgasbord of supernatural phenomena. Startlingly high percentages of people believe in ESP, psychic healing, UFOs, astrology, alien abductions, channeling, and reincarnation. Among those who listen to preaching, more have read *The Celestine Prophecy* or *Conversations with God* or *The Shack* than even the Bible itself. Those to whom we preach are not too skeptical when it comes to religion; rather, they are too gullible.

One of my most intelligent, educated, successful members popped into my office one day, wide eyed, and handed me a book detailing how there is a tenth planet, which scientists have failed to detect, that will pass perilously close to earth in just a few weeks, causing catastrophic destruction. The source of this knowledge? The Bible (naturally) and some Akkadian tablets from Ur, Abraham's homeland. A schoolteacher once asked me, "Will you ever talk to us about your past lives?" Note the plural: *lives*. At an afternoon vesper service, light from the stained-glass window settled on my head, leading a couple (and some deity gave them both the same revelation simultaneously) to hug me afterwards, saying God's spirit was heavily upon me and through that spirit God told them to sell their home and move to Colorado. I wish I could say I was sorry to see them go.

Celebrities are the new authorities in things religious, from Shirley MacLaine to Demi Moore to Della Reese (who played an angel on TV). Celebrities become virtual divinities, from Princess Di to Oprah to Dale Earnhardt. Self-protection or self-indulgence is at the heart of most religious fads, and we must admit up front that ours is not an easy religiosity that pleases base fancies. Deepak Chopra (in *Ageless Body, Timeless Mind*) promises to lead us to a land "where old age, infirmity, and death do not exist and are not even entertained as a possibility," while our Gospel demands we give up everything to follow the Crucified.

GOD ISN'T LISTENING

One earmark of BS may be that it is too flimsy to carry much weight. If you plumb the depths of BS, you discover there simply are no depths. Too many sermons, while they may not be trying to talk anybody into anything, suffer from a sort of theological and psychological "thinness." Simple, easily explained, uncomplicated thoughts are popular in a way, but at the end of the day they cannot carry the freight. They lack the muscle to explain the mystery that is life with God, much less the intersection of the Divine with human darkness.

I am not sure of the best strategy to avoid thin triviality. It may be that a rich life of reading is a cure—and not the "how to preach catchy sermons" books or the "how to run an effective church" books, but those Mark Helprin spoke of, "books that were hard to read, that could devastate and remake one's soul, and that, when they were finished, had a kick like a mule."[6] It may be that a listening heart is the antidote to thin preaching. We watch the news and contemplate the suffering in the world, or we listen to a parishioner devastated by the course of life, or we let ourselves become attentive to the darkness and pain in our own lives, and we compose the sermon out of that place, "out of the depths" from which the Psalmist cried out to God (Ps. 130:1). We let our hearts be broken by the things that break the heart of God, as World Vision's Bob Pierce put it.[7]

Some sermons are pleasant, and I am one who wishes people were more pleasant than they in fact are. But while your mother may have said, "If you cannot say anything nice, don't say anything at all," God would prefer you not apply that pithy thought to preaching. We labor under no obligation to speak always positively, always warmly, always smiling, always uplifting. People ache, and they need the ache to be named before God—and without a rush to reply or fix the ache.

When I was in seminary, I had a close friend who suffered terribly yet courageously from cystic fibrosis. During one particularly bleak night at the Duke Medical Center, I was sitting with her and her mother, agonizing with her as she wearily fought for the most shallow of breaths, desperately unable to stave off the pain. When I stood up to leave, her mother was standing over by the window, looking out at—well, at nothing at all. The panes exposed the blackness of the night, nothing more. Pitifully I asked, "Would you like for me to say a prayer?" Her barely audible reply numbed me: "Pray if you wish. Nobody's listening."

We pastors overhear the awful thunder of such feelings, and we delicately tuck this moment into a sermon. Many sermons shrink back from repeating such a poignant, sorrowful moment. Some preachers I know might repeat the story, but then lunge into some sort of banal corrective: "Oh, but God *is* listening! We know God always listens, we cannot doubt, we must always trust." Sure, God is listening, but we most certainly *can* doubt—and isn't there a kind of trust that can blurt out in misery, "God isn't listening"? What we do with the moment in the sermon can either tenderly shove open a window in the dark or cruelly slam the door. If her words make you shudder and want to run, if you are tempted to fix her, to reverse her doubt, then do not even think of using the story in a sermon. In fact, you might consider getting out of the ministry. When a mother sits in hospital rooms over the years, for months, for weeks, for days, for hours, for even one minute, with her daughter who battles for just some air, she knows the darkness. She knows nobody's listening.

The preacher can at least listen, and go with her agony, feel some small percentage of her anguish, and never rush so swiftly to the "good news" that for this mother cannot be anything but bad news. In the context of the sermon, even though that mother isn't in the room, you must see the people in front of you who appear to be watching and listening to you, and they know. They too have blankly stared out into that darkness. They too believe nobody's listening. Telling the story declares to each one of them, "I know too. I understand. What you feel, what you dread, can exist in this sanctuary, before the God you don't even believe is listening. It's okay." Who are you to fix all the mothers (or even one of them) whose lives have been flayed, whose wounds are gaping, who will cry out against God, with or without you? Didn't Jesus, in the hour in which he revealed God to us most fully, flail out into a dark void, screaming "My God, my God, why have you forsaken me?"

If they hear you, if you join hearts with them to say, "God isn't listening," then they will also be closer to God. How was God revealed most transparently to us? Not in snappy answers, or some snippet Jesus or Paul or Jeremiah allegedly gave to uncomfortable theological questions, not in slamming the iron door shut on any hint of doubt. On the cross, when the glory of God was most truthfully exposed to us, Jesus spoke to God but basically accused God of not listening. What did Jesus see in the gathering darkness, in his isolation and dereliction, from the vantage point of the cross?

We name the ache. We articulate the brokenheartedness. We say what people have not let themselves say out loud, even to themselves, in the course of the week. Under the thinnest possible veneer, people try to cloak a river of tears, a scream of desperation. God knows, God understands, and the preacher says what is not "nice," what cuts to the marrow. And it isn't all up to the preacher. Every text, or just about every text, has some dark pocket of heartbreak somewhere, and the preacher had better find it and name it. Naaman, according to 2 Kings 5:1, is a "great man . . . in high favor . . . a mighty man of valor . . . but he was a leper." There is always a "but," isn't there? And it is the "but," which we hide from others and even ourselves, that nags, weeps, and finally opens the window to grace.

In the long account in John 11 of the raising of Lazarus, the heartbreak comes in verse 21: "If you had been here, my brother would not have died." Lingering in every soul is some "if only . . ." for which God not only must answer but is eager to embrace. Toward the end of Isaiah, God speaks in 65:1: "I was ready to be sought by those who did not ask for me. . . . I said 'Here am I, here am I,' to a nation that did not call on my name." To go unnoticed, to be uninvited, to be unchosen: we know the ache; and in this case, the heartbreak we know mirrors that in God's own heart.

Read Genesis 22 slowly and consider the poignant echoes of the repeated words like "your," "only," "love." Your own soul will shiver, your heart will be rendered helpless before the holy demand and startling grace of God: "Take your son, your only son Isaac, whom you love, and go to the land of Moriah." Then ponder the dialogue between father and son, with the gasping numbness nestled between the lines: "Isaac said to his father Abraham, 'My father!' And he said, 'Here am I, my son.' He said, 'Behold the fire and the wood; but where is the lamb for a burnt offering?'" Where indeed? Then verse 8 adds, "So they went both of them together." The heartbreak. The locus of the Gospel.

SHADOW AND LIGHT

So the preacher must, at all costs, avoid the trite and trivial, or pleasant, sweet thoughts, the type people post on their personal Internet pages or e-mail around. I recall this bungling banality that was being passed around a few years ago—the one about a guy being buried with a fork in his hand. The punch line was that he had enjoyed the "meal" of his life but was hanging on to the fork because he was getting set for "dessert." The story is too trivial to be meaningful, a cake fork simply being unable to carry sufficient weight to cope with the awful burden of death—but then I heard it, out loud, at a funeral where I happened to be sitting next to the widow, one of my employees who'd asked me to be with her. As we exited the church, she leaned into my ear and snarled, "Damn fork story! Jim would never have wanted to go off and have dessert without me." Then she kept venting. "See that woman over there? She told me Jim's in a better place. But I want him here with me."

In my book on *The Will of God*, I reminded readers of an unforgettable moment in the movie *Steel Magnolias*. Shelby, a young mother, has died at age twenty-seven, leaving behind a young son. The mourners are drifting away after the burial, but Shelby's mother, played perfectly by Sally Field, lingers by the grave. Her friends notice and gather to try to offer comfort. Truvy and Clairee say something about how pretty the flowers are, then stare at their shoes in awkward discomfort. Annelle, a young hairdresser who is quite devout, offers solace: "It should make you feel a lot better that Shelby is with her king. We should all be rejoicing." Shelby's mother responds: "Well, you go on ahead. I'm sorry if I don't feel like it. I guess I'm kind of selfish. I'd rather have her here." And then she begins to give voice to her ache, her horror, her total, exasperating agony, screaming from the marrow of her gut: "Why? Why? Why?" Screaming, sobbing, she literally hollers, "Oh God! I want to know Why? Why? Lord, I wish I could understand! It's not supposed to happen this way! I'm supposed to go first! I don't think I can take this!" Moviemaking has seldom portrayed such compelling emotion.

Who was more faithful? Annelle with her very true spiritual statements of faith? Or the mother, casting about in the dark, hurling unanswerable questions, incapable of absorbing what are supposed to be comforting words of faith? Is the preacher obligated to play the part of Annelle? Shouldn't we embody the mother's cry? Can we see that the most lovely benefit of preaching like the mother instead of Annelle might be to help the congregation to learn how to love, to hear the cry of others in the Body of Christ, not to apply a silly salve of trite answers to those who suffer, but to "suffer with those who suffer," thus giving the sufferers permission to grieve, and thus to experience genuine love and grace?

It is hard to say whether Annelle or the fork have simply slimmed the Gospel down too far, or if the Gospel is actually perverted by the attempt at simplicity. We miss the bearable, necessary weight of the Gospel either way. How far are Annelle and the fork from the exemplary, often-quoted (and rightly so), downright poetic and powerful sermon by Frederick Buechner on Jacob's wrestling with a man (or angel, or God) in Genesis 32?

Buechner calls this an "ancient, jagged-edged story" which frankly isn't very edifying. Jacob is strong and ambitious, but longs to go home again. Intuiting more than the text actually tells us, Buechner suggests that the enemy held back through most of the fight, "letting Jacob almost win so that when he was defeated he would know he was truly defeated, so he would know that not all the shrewdness and brute force he could muster were enough to get this." Jacob won't let go, but his grip is more desperation than fighting any longer. Then Buechner cleverly suggests what Jacob finally saw—not the face of death but something more terrible: the face of love. Inevitably we all wind up fighting with God, who demands everything before giving us everything. Buechner's clinching image:

> Remember the last glimpse we have of Jacob, limping home against the dawn. Remember Jesus, staggering on broken feet out of the tomb toward the Resurrection, bearing on his body the proud insignia of the defeat which is victory, the magnificent defeat of the human soul at the hands of God.[8]

No hint here that Christ is the "answer" to our problems, or to our questions. Moralists always want to do the American male thing: fix the problem! But we are called way beyond moralism, beyond "niceness." God did make the world and is involved in all of it, the sweet and the agonizing, smiles and frowns, life and death. Consider in conclusion this extended thought from Karl Barth:

> Light exists as well as shadow. Creation has not only a positive but also a negative side. It belongs to the essence of creaturely nature, and is indeed a mark of its perfection, that it has in fact this negative side. In creation there is not only a Yes but also a No; not only a height but also an abyss; not only clarity but also obscurity; not only growth but also decay; not only opulence but also indigence; not only beauty but also ashes; not only beginning but also end. In the existence of man there are hours, days and years both bright and dark, success and failure, laughter and tears, youth and age, gain and loss, birth and sooner or later its inevitable corollary, death. In all this, creation praises its Creator and Lord even on its shadowy side. For all we can tell, may not His creatures praise Him more mightily in humility than in exaltation, in need than in plenty, in fear than in joy? May not we ourselves praise Him more purely on bad days than on good, more surely in sorrow than in rejoicing, more truly in adversity than in progress? If there may be praise of God from the abyss, night and misfortune . . . how surprised we shall be, and how ashamed of so much unnecessary disquiet and discontent, once we are brought to realize that all creation both as light and shadow, including our own share in it, was laid on Jesus Christ, and that even though we did not see it, while we were shaking our heads that things were not very different, it sang the praise of God just as it was, and was therefore right and perfect.[9]

Truth is light, and dark. Truth sits in the shadow of sorrow and sighs. Truth is easier to tell than we had imagined, for we need no agility, no gymnastic gyrations, to try to string up lights in dark corners. Truth always looks to Jesus—and especially to his cross—and is content in its shadow.

6

Out Loud and Out There

So how would a preacher go about preaching this "light and shadow," voicing this elusive kind of truth that is far from simple and yet utterly simple, true to the gut of real life and the Gospel? To consider this, we turn now to wrestle energetically with a question: Where do sermons really come from? Where do they really happen? Sermons do not "happen" in the study or at a computer, and in a way they don't entirely "happen" in your sanctuary. They happen "out there," they are born and die out there—as we will see. Sermons also happen "in here," in you—not on the surface of your cranium but in some deep place in your soul. We will reflect on the path to that place, which is the same path the sermon takes to that place in the listeners and is also the same path God took in coming to us in Christ.

Before we go there, let us declare: sermons happen "out loud." It is a common but lamentable mistake to think that a sermon is something that is "written." You may use a pen or a keyboard to gather what you want to say, but a sermon is something that is spoken—obviously! Yet how much energy is expended, and how frequently does the communication break down, because we begin by writing, and then try to transform black and white words on a page into something oral? Do we memorize? Do we glance up and down, like a bobbing-head figurine, trying to pretend we don't have paper? Why am I fairly interesting to my friends when we're sitting around the kitchen table, but comparatively dull standing behind a pulpit? How can it be that I have so many really cool theological ideas, but they don't get past some thick invisible shield that seems to be propped between me and those who watch and listen to me?

Sermons begin out loud. In sermon preparation, talk out loud for a good while before you think about jotting or typing. We will get back to that. For now, let's explore the entire nature of spoken communication, why it works, the way it is so beautiful, where the breakdowns occur, and why visuals, PowerPoint, video clips, and big screens—which probably have their place—are risky business and can never replace the essence of preaching, which has always been and will always be something that happens out loud, face to face: words that matter exchanged between people.

But words seem so cheap, there are too many words, they do not seem potent enough. Probing the peculiarities of preaching in the modern Church, Jürgen Moltmann has tried to diagnose the difficulty we bump up against when we frame the Word of God in words:

> Much has been written about the crisis of language in general and the crisis of preaching in particular, at a time when we are flooded with words in public and are personally inarticulate. People have lamented the powerlessness of language in a period where words are not supposed to decide anything.[1]

Caving in to our visually titillating culture, preachers have forgotten how to trust the spoken word and have erected screens in the sanctuary to flash images devised to cope with ever-shortening attention spans and optimistically to "show" what we need to "say." But theologically, wasn't Martin Luther right when he argued that the organ of faith is never the eye, but the ear, relying on texts like "We walk by faith, not by sight" (2 Cor. 5:7), "Faith is . . . the conviction of things not seen" (Heb. 11:1), "Faith comes from what is heard, and what is heard comes by the preaching of Christ" (Rom. 10:17)? David Steinmetz has captured this sentiment profoundly:

> The God who reveals himself in the pages of Holy Scripture is a God who works contrary to human expectation. The work of God is therefore not visible to sight, since everything the eye sees provides impressive grounds for distrusting the promises of God. The eye sees weakness not strength, folly not wisdom, humiliation not victory. Consequently Luther pits the ear against the eye. The Christian must hear by faith the promise which runs contrary to the empirical evidence his eye can assess and trust it.[2]

Later we will balance Luther's passion for the ear by comparing the way writers from Ephrem the Syrian to Ignatius Loyola and others have spoken of an inner, spiritual, "luminous" eye that ratchets the imagination so we might visually perceive the things of God.

LAZY VIEWERS

Now we will touch on two other holes into which we will tumble if we neglect the auditory, the sheer power of words. First, let us consider the advent of television and its impact on sports, which the average fan would assess positively. Mel Allen, who broadcast New York Yankees games on radio and then television, lamented the rise of television, feeling it rendered his words extraneous. He decided that television was "a medium in which both the broadcaster and the fan became lazy—the broadcaster because he had to let the camera do so much of the work and the fan because he did not have to use his imagination. Allen felt he had a less-intimate relationship with his viewers."[3] Allen's "soft, almost silky voice . . . brought the fan into the Stadium . . . and projected a sense of intimacy with the players."

> He would begin by painting a word portrait. . . . Television would be different in many ways, not least of all for the athletes. In the beginning it seemed to bring them greater fame, but in time it became clear that the fame was not so much greater as quicker. More often than not, it evaporated sooner. As radio was an instrument that could heighten the mystique of a player, television eventually demythologized the famous.[4]

This plaintive nostalgia may rekindle in us a high vision of what might go on in the preaching moment. Some brakes must be applied on lives that are ever quicker; the sermon cannot and would not dare keep pace with the dizzying rush people know. We invite people to slow down, to combat their spiritual laziness by a slow labor that requires some effort, some mental energy. Imagination is required, of the preacher and of the listener. We do not make it too easy or too simple for them; we guard some mystique, painting word portraits that simultaneously expose the mystique for a moment, but then we throw a cloak back over what always remains mystery. We create that intimacy wrought only by words. We trust the beauty of the spoken word.

A soft, silky voice is not so important as loving attention to words—and loving invitations to use the imagination, not "showing" what we want to say, but letting the words do their work in the inner being of the listener, who grows by listening, not watching. We have practitioners out there who dazzle us with words, and we are wise to go and do likewise. For instance, Rowan Williams, in a real sermon to real people, said, "Christmas is a beauty that is the beginning of terror: the Burning Babe, who has come to cast fire upon the earth. Before his presence, the idols fall and shatter."[5] How lovely—although you may wonder if the ear can comprehend a sustained sermon with this kind of verbiage. Williams, after all, preached this in the cathedral in Oxford, while you and I find ourselves standing before farmers in Iowa, or factory workers in Pittsburgh, or bored teenagers.

Wherever we find ourselves, we bear the burden of choosing words with care. James Weldon Johnson crafted eloquent sermons in the earthiest dialect, and I know a rural preacher with no obvious stage presence who quite brilliantly can turn words like "y'all" and even twists of incorrect grammar into a surgeon's probing scope that brings healing to the soul. I suspect that preachers, in our dumbed down culture, have a peculiar obligation to keep the English language alive. If I don't use words people still vaguely know, like "cacophony" and "foment," "gregarious" and "quarrel," "fastidious" and "malevolent," no one else who talks out there will keep them alive, and God must be a lover of words to have become the Word. Words we use with tender care; they are like our very young children, and we caress them and show them off to anybody who will listen.

FIVE MOST BEAUTIFUL MOMENTS

Even more to the point, when weighing the importance of preaching "out loud," to draw very close to the heart of what can and might happen in the preaching moment, consider this question: "What do you consider to be the five most beautiful moments of your life?" If we ask this of ourselves, friends, colleagues, church folks, or family, we rush for a few seconds to something that is "pretty," like a sunrise over the ocean or wildflowers in a meadow.

But press further, give the question a little time, and we all begin to remember beautiful moments that involve words being spoken face to face with someone who matters. In my top five I would include the evening, when I was a single clergyman, when I prepared a candle-light dinner of chicken and stuffed mushrooms for Lisa. This was to be not just any night, but hopefully the turning point from mere dating to something more lasting. We ate, and then I serenaded her at the piano. I cannot be sure, but I suspect that the entire membership of my Church had circled the parsonage in a prayer vigil, so determined were they to marry me off. Finally, I took my life in my hands and declared to her as firmly yet tenderly as possible: "I love you." No cuisine, no serenading could guarantee what her reply might be. She could have squirmed and muttered, "Uh, well, you're a nice guy, but . . ." Instead, she gently graced my trembling future by nodding, "I love you too."

This story is illustrative of quite a number of truths, but this moment is also beautiful, and perhaps even revelatory. The beauty resides not merely in the happy conclusion to the story. The beauty of the moment emerges out of the utter vulnerability of the lover, for beauty teeters on the edge of darkness. When you tell someone, "I love you," you forsake all control, you abandon self-protection. You take this marvelous, fragile crystal of your self and hand it to another person, who might drop you, and you watch your self being shattered into pieces that can never quite be glued back together; or the beloved might cradle your lovely self to her breast. There is something we forget in the midst of virtually every beautiful moment: when you celebrate a newfound love, when you utter and absorb words that matter and thus the world changes, some door slams shut behind you. Dizzy with what is transpiring before you, you may not hear the door slam, but later you realize that something got foreclosed on you.

Should the preacher relate such a personal story? Maybe, maybe not. We may be emboldened to do so, if we recall that I am not relating information about myself to people because I foolishly think they should take some interest in my history. Rather, the story I tell is not particular to me. Everyone with a pulse has handed her crystalline self to someone. Every person knows he has been broken a time or two. Every person hopefully has been cradled by another. Frederick Buechner is a modern master of such stories, in those autobiographical books whose very titles are invitations to enter *A Room Called Remember*, to engage in *Telling Secrets*, to hatch a *Memoir of Early Days*, to discover we are all *Longing for Home*; the preacher must become adept at *Listening to Your Life*. Buechner remembers and tells of his life, not so that we can be voyeurs and gather biographical information. The moments of his life awaken memories of our own lives, and we begin to discover together that life with God is played out in such moments or not at all. So the stories we nurture are not just analogies, not just illustrations, but work in the way Hans-Georg Gadamer describes poetry: "Ordinary language resembles a coin that we pass around among ourselves in place of something else, whereas poetic language is like gold itself."[6] Revelatory moments are not just coin, but gold: God's work, God's presence, vocation dawning, self discovered, truth told.

The truth is not always pretty, but the truth is always beautiful. "Pretty" is too objective, too much about taste. "Pretty" is unalloyed sweetness that I prefer for my own pleasure. Beauty entails risk, vulnerability. Rainer Maria Rilke hauntingly wrote that beauty is

> the beginning of terror, which we can just barely endure,
> and we stand in awe of it as it coolly disdains
> to destroy us. Every angel is terrifying.[7]

When we dare to get close to beauty, when we dare to get close to truth, when we dare to get close to God, there is terror, the prospect of being shattered, of losing everything. Artists and musicians know this, as the greatest compositions explore deftly that unfenced border between love and loss, between light and darkness, between delight and pain.

Beautiful moments, revelatory moments, need not all be positive. Preaching that is beautiful must venture into what is ugly, what is not pretty, touching wounds, knowing listeners will recoil, remembering the shrewd adage of Tolkien's wise old Gandalf, who in a letter reminded Frodo Baggins that "all that is gold does not glitter."[8] Notice he does not say, "All that glitters is not gold," for then we would only sift through what glitters in our quest for the gold. No, "all that is gold does not glitter."

Hence a second beautiful moment from my own life, and again we hear words that matter being exchanged. The telephone rang out in the night. Hurry! Now! He's very ill. My grandfather, Papa Howell, the epitome of whatever delight and goodness filled my childhood, my hero and best friend, was so ill that my aunt phoned at such an hour. We piled into the car and drove hard for hours, silently, along the road we had traversed so many times filled with joyful anticipation. Not long after dawn, we finally pulled up in front of the house. We just sat, as if paralyzed, as my father turned off the car, opened the door, and somberly walked up to his brothers, who were standing under the giant oak tree where we had all played and churned ice cream a hundred times. My sister and I could not hear what was said, but we saw my dad and his brothers fall on each other's shoulders, and they cried out loud. This was in the mid-sixties, and my dad and uncles were all strong, immovable military men. I can still hear their wailing.

A beautiful moment, however sad. The death of the beloved, knee-buckling, yet beautiful. For in that moment we children learned that life is precious, that love is intense, that a life could matter so much. There is a beauty hidden in grief. Love unfailingly plunges you into excruciating agony, but we would not think for a moment of loving any less. By analogy we could say, "God's love is like that." And so it is. God's love costs God and costs us everything, and tears are shed. But the Gospel is not merely illustrated by this moment of my grandfather's death. God was under those trees and in my gut, as God is always palpable when God's children suffer but manage to stand and take another breath. In grown men's sobbing we overhear God's own lament. In a child's stricken agony we are enveloped by the heart of God.

The sermon lives off these moments of beauty, these revelatory memories and happenings. It is not enough for the sermon to be exegetically correct and theologically sound. The sermon may rise to the level of beauty, for it is only beauty that can lure us toward God, it is only beauty that is appropriate to God, who is beauty.

TALK, DON'T WRITE

So, if you love, and have some truth that isn't too corrupted by BS, how do you love the people out there who hear you talking out loud? You prepare out loud, and take more seriously than we often do that they are, quite literally, "out there." Sermons do not happen sitting at a desk with commentaries splayed in front of the preacher, in the splendid isolation of the Church study. There are couple of reasons for this.

First, is it is simply too quiet in there. Don't turn on iTunes, but there must be sound, since a sermon is sound. Talk out loud long before you type. Pick a text, listen to it out loud in the car perhaps, or read it aloud, muse a bit; and if there is anything in that text that is intriguing, then start talking about it—to the cat in the corner, to your spouse, to a colleague, to a doorknob. Anything or anybody will do. Imagine somebody walks in off the street and says, "What is your text for Sunday?" You tell them, you open the Bible and read it for them. Then they ask you, "Gosh, what on earth would you say about that? What's that passage about?" You wouldn't turn to the computer and type quietly. You would say something. You might stammer and ramble a bit, but you would be talking, which is what you'll be required to do come Sunday. Prepare out loud. The "writing" is only note taking and refining what is first and last an "out loud" encounter. In his popular text on preaching, *Just Say the Word! Writing for the Ear*, Robert Jacks helped a new wave of preachers realize we compose something that is first and finally an out loud event.

Second, mining commentaries may be essential background labor, but it is a futile and frustrating exercise to have a text to preach upon, and then to rifle through a commentary to find what some scholar said about this passage and think a sermon that brings God directly to bear on the guy in the fourth pew will emerge. Partly, the commentaries fastidiously strive for objectivity and linger back in the first century, or expend much creative energy on what was hypothetically "behind" the text. We need to know what they try to teach us! But we need to know it more thoroughly than a mere passage check can bear. When we hunt up a given text and see what even a solid commentary has to say, we may be like the student who forever holds a multiplication table or a calculator in hand to solve each problem. Four times five? Let's see: ah, twenty! Three times six? Hmm . . . Found it! Eighteen. But you never get the feel of the numbers or understand their inherent relationships. Know the Scriptures, more than this isolated text. Remember that this text is a mere window into a larger castle, and the labor to know not just Mark 1:46–52 but all of Mark 1, all of Mark, all of the New Testament, and all of Scripture must be done in advance of the sermon on Mark 1:46–52.

GET A LIFE OUT THERE

The larger reason commentaries don't cough up sermons is that you probe them in an office in the Church, and that is not where the people to whom you speak have spent any time that week. You spend hours "in here," or in other unnatural settings like a hospital or nursing home or homeless shelter or Christian bookstore. But the people you speak to have been in natural settings like an office tower, a factory, a bar, a movie theater, or in the den watching TV, or stalled in traffic. If that is where they have lived, and if that is where we fantasize that they might some day know and connect with God, then perhaps we should not only go to the same places, but even "write" sermons there. Get outside, and do that talking out loud in a park or strolling downtown. Get out of the Church and explain the text to an imaginary passenger in your car while stalled in traffic. Watch a TV show with the Bible on your lap, and tell one of the characters in the show what you're planning to say on Sunday. Vincent van Gogh, who was a preacher before he devoted himself entirely to art, once wrote that "I have sometimes had a lesson from a German reaper that was of more use to me than one in Greek."[9] Look at his *Potato Eaters* (1885), peasants eating by candlelight a meager meal dug with their own hands, and you will see those about whom we speak in the sermon.

There's an old saw you may have heard that is a bit impolite, but revealing. A student asks a professor, "How can I preach more interesting sermons?" The professor answers, "Get a more interesting life." Get out from behind the desk, go bowling, hang out with strangers, surf the Internet, try foreign food. The more the preacher is immersed in the life of the world, the more the sermon will be able to make that unfailingly intriguing connection between the Gospel and real life. If you get bored at a movie or by cocktail party conversation, then good! You're on your way to preaching a sermon that is, by comparison, titillating.

The interesting preacher is well immersed in this world, but gives clear (even if subtle) evidence of having withdrawn and reflected upon the world and upon the things of God. Our task (or privilege) is to live fully in the world, but in a manner that reflects subtly yet seductively that we have indulged in prayer and reflection, that we have spent time apart from the world with God, so that we comprehend how God is present in the realities of the real world, how God is manifest where our parishoners live when they are out in the parish. By our rhythm of immersion and withdrawal, and by our honesty in telling about it, we draw those who are watching toward a vantage point where they too may discover that God is in their lives and that their lives are immersed in God.

And don't forget to run a little inventory on the company you keep. Whom do you know? If you only know sweet Church people who naturally gravitate to the clergy, your preaching will be vapid. Golf with a neighbor who despises Church, not to try to convert him on the thirteenth hole, but to listen—or just to play golf and become a broader person. Do whatever it takes to befriend somebody whose skin color is different from yours, somebody who digs spiritualities you think are weird, somebody who isn't from where you're from, maybe a rabbi or an imam. You can learn from such people. Ask a restaurateur how to run a restaurant, and you'll preach better. Ask a songwriter how to make lyrics work. Ask an entrepreneur how to run a business. Ask an atheist what he thinks of the text you're carrying around with you. Get out of the office, get out of the Church, and write—or ruminate, chat, and jot down notes—out there.

THE NOTICED LIFE

Think once more about beautiful moments. Not many have happened for me while my nose has been buried in a commentary. I love commentaries, and I need their corrective discipline, to yoke my self securely to the text, to keep me from meandering away into a sermon that is little more than my trivial thoughts about life or, worse, my private prejudices about the arrangement of the universe. The preacher must do her homework, must know the books; but the sermon isn't hiding in the library. The sermon is out there in the world, where God is active, the crucial place where the listener in the pew will respond to the sermon, the place where life with God happens or doesn't happen.

So we have to get out of the office and get our antennae up, probing life for whatever it will give up today. There is plenty out there, but we have to pay attention. Since we perhaps haven't been paying close attention, we need a guide, a mentor (or two or three). Annie Dillard is a marvelous docent, teaching us how to go out into the world and notice the wonder of a penny on the sidewalk or a bug climbing on a leaf. After watching a mockingbird swooping downward repeatedly for several minutes, she compares his free fall to "the old philosophical conundrum about the tree that falls in the forest. The answer must be, I think, that beauty and grace are performed whether or not we will or sense them. The least we can do is try to be there."[10]

Rather delightfully, she tells of growing up in Pittsburgh. When she was six or seven,

> I used to take a precious penny of my own and hide it for someone else to find. I would cradle it at the roots of a sycamore, say, or in a hole left by a chipped-off piece of sidewalk. Then I would take a piece of chalk, and, starting at either end of the block, draw huge arrows leading up to the penny from both directions. After I learned to write I labeled the arrows: SURPRISE AHEAD or MONEY THIS WAY. I was greatly excited, during all this arrow-drawing, at the thought of

the first lucky passer-by who would receive in this way, regardless of merit, a free gift from the universe. . . . The world is fairly studded and strewn with pennies cast broadside from a generous hand. But—and this is the point—who gets excited by a mere penny? . . . But if you cultivate a healthy poverty and simplicity, so that finding a penny will literally make your day, then, since the world is in fact planted in pennies, you have with your poverty bought a lifetime of days.[11]

Or a lifetime of sermons? We are angling for simplicity here. We stretch way back, bang ourselves on the head to knock the clatter of adult clutter out of our noggins, and recall how as children we got excited about pennies and chalk arrows. Beauty is out there, and even up there. A little stargazing, or borrowing a telescope to inspect the moons around Saturn wouldn't do the preacher any harm. But beauty is also back there, where we grew up. Admittedly, a steady diet of sermons about the preacher's childhood could give a congregation indigestion.

Go out to your car, and climb in the back seat. Fidget for a minute or two, and then turn around—yes, on your knees. Look out the back window, and remember. The engine hums as you look back on the road you steadily leave behind. What happened along the way? What mattered? What hurt? What makes you grin? Where is the spot, way back there, you would eagerly pony up your life savings to revisit?

Under that same old oak tree where my father and his brothers wept at my grandfather's death, we used to churn ice cream in the gathering afternoon shade. Mama Howell would prepare her milk, peach, chocolate, sugar concoction; my sister would carefully shimmy chunks of ice down into the perimeter of the churn, lacing the ice with salt; and Papa Howell would sit on a little wooden chair and turn the crank. Filled with expectation, I was surprised, eager, a little hesitant, when Papa Howell summoned me to the task: "Whew, I'm getting' a little tired. . . . James, come over here and help me." He hoisted me over his knee and into his lap, and I cockily grasped the handle, and pushed with all my might. His hand rested on mine, strongly, helping in that gentle way that you don't notice until you're grown, turning, turning, turning again, the voice of praise right in my ear, "Good job, good job."

Just a good story? Or maybe an analogy, an illustration, of how God uses us, helping us? Or is there more? Wasn't that moment in itself a precious gift of God's grace? Not just to me, but to you? When I remember, doesn't it help you to remember? I once heard one of my preaching colleagues tell of one of those long nights when his child wrestled with a fever. Having plied him with Tylenol, having been yo-yoed in and out of the room, Michael went in to check once more and asked, "Do you need anything?" His son said, "Daddy, I just need you in here." And I remembered my Sarah, fighting I suppose the same sort of fever, making that same appeal: "Daddy, I just need you in here." And I remembered wanting my own parents to stay with me in the dark, just to be with me.

The remembering and telling of such stories can be fruitful, although perils lurk. When the preacher relates some moment from her life, she must do so humbly, not forgetting for one second that the story is a big chalk arrow pointing away from the preacher toward the listener, toward God. The story has to fill that Cyrano de Bergerac role of passing messages between lovers, with the preacher playing the midwife for others who may be all too willing to be voyeurs instead of participants. The story must build a bridge, and be accessible. I once heard a preacher tell this torturous tale of how he was in the state finals of the hundred-yard dash; although he started poorly, he mustered the strength needed to pass the competition and break the tape as a champion. Perhaps that congregation was thrilled, but since God, without explanation, made me flat-footed and slow, I felt nothing but distance from this preacher and his message, as he left me too in the dust.

Buechner, by sharing his memories, has prodded many of us to poke around in our own memories. How fascinating is it that he can tell (as he does in several books) the story of his father's suicide, and those of us with living fathers are still moved? His loss breaks your heart, because somewhere in the back of your soul you always suspect that life really is fragile and even those who love you could leave you. That his father left but yours stayed bears considerable weight. Buechner's assumption is "that the story of any one of us is in some measure the story of us all."[12] You have had your own hurts, anyhow, as has every person who ever slides into a pew. Without overindulging your own ego, risk sharing something that happened out there, and thus in the depths of your being. Buechner explains:

> I suppose, it is like looking through someone else's photograph album. What holds you, if nothing else, is the possibility that somewhere among all those shots of people you never knew and places you never saw, you may come across something or someone you recognize.[13]

The stories we tell cannot be all sweetness and light. Some moments we notice and relate are unspeakably dark. We spoke earlier of my grandfather's death and of the young woman dying of cystic fibrosis and her mother's palpable certainty that God was no longer listening. It is in the place where God isn't listening that resurrection happens, that grace becomes palpable. Jesus—bruised, bleeding, despised and rejected, bearing our griefs, carrying our sorrows, wounded for our transgressions, with no comeliness, no beauty that we should desire him—is the one truly beautiful one. Beautiful Savior. Preaching about this cruciform beauty, pointing like John the Baptist to the decimated one who for once fully exhibits the unspeakable beauty that is the heart of God, is possible, and can be enhanced—once we think through how to execute that nettlesome challenge in the art of homiletics: the dreaded, but essential, "illustration."

7

Secular Parables and Saints

In Martin Luther King Jr.'s sermon "How the Christian Overcomes Evil" the featured illustration, from mythology no less, is about the sirens and Ulysses and Orpheus. We admire King's dazzling ingenuity at finding just the right illustration, the unforgettable image, and we are forever on the prowl for this kind of material. Step back and contemplate his strategy, which we know all too well. Usually we take up the text, engage in careful exegesis, discover the "point" of that text (and that text alone), and then perhaps hunt for an illustration, some story or anecdote that "illustrates" the "point." Charles Haddon Spurgeon illustrated the need for illustrations by speaking of the need for windows "to let light in to illuminate the house"; "a building without windows would be a prison rather than a house."[1]

Isn't our urge to extract and package a simple "point" nothing more than our desire to control and manage a biblical text that would prefer to be itself? What is the point of a poem, or, in Scripture, a Psalm? What is the point of a parable? If the point of the parable of the Prodigal Son is something like "God never stops loving you," then why didn't Jesus just cut to the quick and say, "God never stops loving you"? Was it because real life doesn't feel like "points"? If I ask you to tell me about yourself, you are not likely to reel off a dozen points that summarize your existence. Instead, you tell a story, you paint a picture. What is the point of a painting, or the point of a symphony?

I wonder if our quest for the point compels us to spend too much time behind closed office doors with our noses in books, when we really should get outside, or perhaps into the art gallery or the symphony hall (or even a country-western bar if your tastes veer that way). The artist teaches us to see. The composer teaches us to listen. Immersing ourselves in the rich life of the world, and paying attention to what is being said between the lines, may not seem at first blush to be the most productive way to grab hold of a sermon idea.

If we can discard the well-worn model of preaching that hikes from exegesis to the point, then illustrations might fall by the wayside. We may over time chuckle about the need to illustrate some truth that resides only in that single text. Instead, the preacher is always looking for revelatory moments, incidents in life, during the week, encounters, memories, which do not make the point of the text so much as they reveal God's presence in the world. How risky are our illustrations? I know people who delight in a certain preacher because of his catchy stories, his memorable anecdotes, which illustrate . . . well, what do they illustrate? The illustrations become the model, the focus, the overheard truth of the sermon, and the better the illustrations, the more likely the Gospel is to be cloaked by the catchy illustration.

OTHER TRUE WORDS ALONGSIDE THE ONE WORD

In a remarkable section of *Church Dogmatics*, Karl Barth spoke of parables in the secular order—a startling notion, coming from one who warned modernity of the dangers of natural theology. True words about God are found not just in Scripture, but even outside the walls of the Church, even through those who know nothing of Christ. How could this be? Barth speculates that Jesus Christ "must have encountered in some way those who speak these words."

> He must have ordained, awakened and called them to take His Word on their lips in the form of witness to Him. It must have pleased the Word of God to allow itself to be in some sense reflected and reproduced in the words of these men.[2]

Barth's warrant is the way Jesus fashioned parables ("little stories which it seems anyone might tell of ordinary human happenings"):

Under his hand, recounted by Jesus, these everyday happenings become what they were not before, and what they cannot be in and of themselves. . . . The New Testament parables are as it were the prototype of the order in which there can be other true words alongside the one Word of God.[3]

Such words must be in "material agreement" with the Word of God. But this miracle happens; even in Scripture, witnesses to the truth frequently emerge from "the darkness of the nations . . . outside the community."

> The community is not Atlas bearing the burden of the whole world on its shoulders. For all its dedication to the cause which it represents in the world, the cause is not its own, nor does the triumph of this cause depend upon it. But the One who has particularly entrusted His cause to it will see to it that it is not left to its own resources in championing it. Even within the world which opposes it, He will ensure that . . . there will be raised up witnesses to its cause.[4]

We can actually count on such parables presenting themselves to us in the mundane, sinful life of the world, because Christ humbly entered that life and reconciled it to God.

If Barth is onto something about this "miraculous" happening of words and events in the life of the world, how might our preaching preparation be refocused and perhaps enriched? What if the preacher got out of the office and watched and listened for these parables and reported them, serving almost as a docent, leading the congregation on a tour of God's world that begins through the window of Scripture but explores all of our life here? What we are gravitating toward now are moments that on first blush might illustrate a preaching text, but they are more than merely illustrative. We are inching toward those moments that are revelatory, that uncover the truth about God and our lives, moments that render a tantalizing glimpse of beauty, even the beauty of life with God.

Remember when we spoke of the "most beautiful moments." These are surely revelatory moments as well. Listen to your own life, listen to the lives of members of the Body of Christ, listen to the life of the world out there, and notice, envision, overhear the presence of God, the hidden activity of the Spirit.

Buechner, regarded by many as the master of the illustration, the real life story that somehow captures the heart of the text at hand, wasn't just talking about chipper moments from childhood when he observed that "all theology, like all fiction, is at its heart autobiography."

> What a theologian is doing essentially is examining as honestly as he can the rough-and-tumble of his own experience with all its ups and downs, its mysteries and loose ends, and expressing . . . the truths about human life and about God that he believes he has found implicit there. . . . If God speaks to us at all in this world, if God speaks anywhere, it is into our personal lives that he speaks. Someone we love dies, say. Some unforeseen act of kindness or cruelty touches the heart or makes the blood run cold. We fail a friend, or a friend fails us, and we are appalled at the capacity we all of us have for estranging the very people in our lives we need the most. Or maybe nothing extraordinary happens at all—just one day following another, helter-skelter, in the manner of days. We sleep and dream. We wake. We work. We remember and forget. And into the thick of it . . . God speaks.[5]

Do we then let this week's lectionary text just slide on down the hill and vanish behind personal life? Hardly. Our focus is always on the text, but that text is a window into what God is doing in our lives and in the life of the world. That text is an imaginative foil against which we pay attention. That text is the lens through which we truly see what we see and hear what we hear.

If Barth was right about those secular parables, then we need not be too dumbfounded when the Holy Spirit miraculously wrests some moment, some word uttered in the rough-and-tumble of life, and like some clever ventriloquist, uses words and transforms them into the Word. A few years ago I was pecking at my computer keyboard, in the throes of trying to devise a sermon for the Sunday prior to Christmas. My week was slipping by, and nothing was happening amid the sprawl of books and much grimacing. My five-year old son, Noah, kept playing in the room, showing me toys, grabbing at my arm, making bizarre noises. Finally (and it is embarrassing to tell you what happened next), in exasperation I said, "Son, you just have to get out of here; Dad has so much work to do." Noah responded very calmly, but with words that worked some violence in my soul: "Okay, Daddy, I'll leave. I don't mean to annoy you." As I turned to see him walking out, I saw myself walking away from that same spot, but thirty-nine years earlier.

I shut off the computer and my foolish busy-ness, went into the attic, and pulled out two grey Red Ball moving boxes. Inside were wads of newspaper—the *Philadelphia Inquirer*, dated October 15, 1964. A huge photo of Nikita Khrushchev, a box score with Johnny Unitas's stats, an ad for a Rambler. Nestled in the crumbling paper were chunks of metal track, then a caboose, an engine, a cattlecar—the Lionel train set my parents gave me for Christmas in 1960, when I was five. Midway through connecting some of the track, Noah ambled into the room. His eyes flew wide open. "Daddy, what is this?" "This was my train, when I was a little boy, like you—and now it's our train, together." He was duly impressed, and after a few minutes, he exclaimed, "This is the coolest toy ever. I bet this train cost a hundred dollars!" I was tempted for 1.3 seconds to calculate the value of those Lionel cars at auction—but instead I told the truth: "Oh no, son. It didn't cost a hundred dollars. It was free."

A busy man. A son rejected. Digging into a box, sharing. It was free. Again, we could say that this moment illustrates some Gospel truth. But there is more. Did God not co-opt my little boy's words to call me out of my frenetic self? And did my reporting his words not in turn call a few other men and women out of their frenetic selves?

BEAUTY MAKING A SPECTACLE OF ITSELF

It would be fruitful to spend time thinking about the impact of art, sculpture, architecture, and music on preaching. Preachers may not feel cultured enough to dwell on this, and we may feel a bit uneasy with all this talk of beauty in art, sculpture, and architecture. There is a tradition of iconoclasm inherent in Judaism and Christianity. On Mount Sinai, God warned Moses about graven images, and Church officials have fretted over the role of art ever since. But the popular need for iconography, the appeal of stained glass, the thrill of a looming nave have won out. The stories of Scripture have been painted, sculpted, sung, dramatized—and always will be—for Scripture is replete with beautiful moments that fire the imaginations of artists. Consider the efforts of those medieval illuminators of Scripture, who not only assiduously copied the text by hand, but added those colorful capital letters to open a book, those intricate images of a character or scene, not to mention the bindings, themselves works of art. The preacher's task is akin to those medieval illuminators, repeating the ancient stories, drawing out the color, calling attention to the wonder, dressing the text up in finery. As we think back to the Middle Ages, we may suggest that the most lovely illumination of the Scriptures may be found in the lives of the saints.

Artists through history have painted the lives of saints, and their lives are beautiful, not so much because they make a point, but because they become a window into the heart of God, a shimmering vision of life with God. The lives of the saints are not illustrative of the Gospel. Rather, in a palpable way they *are* the Gospel, in the sense of God's Word coming to life down on this planet. If the preacher lives and thrives, however perilously, in that mysterious region between the Scripture and the listener, if the preacher is indeed like Cyrano de Bergerac, ferrying notes between two would-be lovers, and if those notes are descriptions of what the preacher has noticed, little snapshots of the grace of God getting its feet under real people down here, then the beauty of preaching will be manifest when we relate moments from the lives of the saints.

John Navone has written that beauty is "goodness making a spectacle of itself so that it may be loved."[6] One spectacle of goodness after another, the perfect love notes passed between God and us mortals are the stories of saints: the official, canonized saints of the Church, but also other heroes of the faith, some from distant lands and times, others whom we may have observed up close in our own circle. As we measure our approach to the beauty of the lives of saints in our preaching, let us begin with the greatest (and most frequently painted) saint of the Middle Ages and then leap to women and men of modern times, to see not merely what the preacher can ferret out to use in a sermon, but also how these saints might forever alter the imagination of those of us who step into pulpits.

St. Francis of Assisi has been the subject of countless books you could read, but for centuries most Catholics knew of his life through art. The most famous frescoes narrating the life of Francis were crafted by Giotto (or at least his "school"). Another painter, van Gogh, when he vacated the pulpit and began to absorb what painters were about, admired Giotto above all the rest: "Giotto moved me most—always in pain, and always full of kindness and enthusiasm, as though he were already living in a different world from ours."[7] We might say he perceived things differently in our world.

As tourists gaze at that pictorial narrative in the great nave of the basilica where Francis is buried, they perceive that the life of Francis was so striking, so lovely, that it had to be captured not just in words but in vibrant color. Each moment of the saint's life (Christ speaking to him at San Damiano, donating exotic fabric to a beggar, teaching the birds, his body seared with the stigmata) is one of those beautiful moments when the Scripture is not woodenly recited, but creatively embodied. The way Francis lived is alluring, attractive, hopeful, in a way that is frankly attainable.

G. K. Chesterton, noting how Francis of Assisi sought to fashion himself after Christ, how Francis was "a most sublime approximation to his Master," "a splendid and yet a merciful Mirror of Christ," shrewdly suggested that

> if St. Francis was like Christ, Christ was to that extent like St. Francis. And my present point is that it is really very enlightening to realise that Christ was like St. Francis. What I mean is this; that if men find certain riddles and hard sayings in the story of Galilee, and if they find the answers to those riddles in the story of Assisi, it really does show that a secret has been handed down in one religious tradition and no other. It shows that the casket that was locked in Palestine can be unlocked in Umbria; for the Church is the keeper of the keys. . . . Now in truth while it has always seemed natural to explain St. Francis in the light of Christ, it has not occurred to many people to explain Christ in the light of St. Francis. . . . St. Francis is the mirror of Christ rather as the moon is the mirror of the sun. The moon is much smaller than the sun, but it is also much nearer to us; and being less vivid it is more visible. Exactly in the same sense St. Francis is nearer to us, and being a mere man like ourselves is in that sense more imaginable.[8]

At first blush, listeners will feel inclined to dismiss the saints, perhaps gawking at them as somehow genetically superior to the rest of us, suspecting that their superhuman feats are unattainable. But hidden in this notion that "Oh, she is a saint" is a ploy to keep our distance, to hold on to our old, two-bit lives. The preacher's challenge, and the preacher's marvelous opportunity, is to debunk this notion, to bridge the gulf, by lifting up the lives of the saints in ways that are compelling.

The saints compel because they *are* just like you and me. The difference, quite simply, is that when the saints read the Bible, they naively thought they were supposed to go out and do it. St. Francis took the Bible literally, not in the sense of rigidly decreeing that God created the world in six twenty-four-hour days, but in the sense of taking the Bible at its word and getting busy with it. The sermon should settle for no less. In our Cyrano de Bergerac guise, we really do want those lovers to get together and for lives to be changed. We do not want applause for the sermon. We want our brothers and sisters to hear the text and let it take on flesh this afternoon, tomorrow morning, next Thursday night.

Dorothy Day wrought a profound interpretation of the gospel from her Fifteenth Street apartment in New York. She read Jesus' charge to the disciples when faced with the hungry five thousand, "You give them something to eat" (Mark 6:37), quite literally. Day took on hunger, serving mulligan stew, bread, and coffee from the front of her flat to hundreds off the street. But she also took on systemic injustice, particularly in the church, publishing—from the back of her flat—the *Catholic Worker*. Its first edition carried these words from Peter Maurin, Dorothy's partner in the paper: "Christ drove the moneychangers out of the Temple. But today nobody dares to drive the money lenders out of the Temple. And nobody dares to drive the money lenders out of the Temple because the money lenders have taken a mortgage on the Temple." The episode in John 2 and Mark 11 is much discussed in terms of the "historical Jesus," but for Day it was an episode to be repeated today and every day, whenever holy precincts become a caricature of themselves.[9]

Sometimes saints are close at hand, if we are fortunate. The best story I know about anyone's piety is about my grandfather. More than a few times in my childhood, as I bounded about his house, I opened a door without knocking and caught my grandfather on his knees, wellworn Bible open before him, in deep prayer, blushing a bit, wishing he'd not been disturbed, but loving me all the same. This sort of piety requires no explanation and is in fact its own explanation, and a tantalizing possibility for me, and for you, once I've named it.

What fascinates us about the saints is that they are exactly like us in constitution and temperament, intelligence and capability, and also in the laughable ways they fail to be as holy as they are so eager to be. Through history, Christians have zealously striven to "imitate" Christ, and valiantly so. But the very notion of "imitation" has a negative connotation or two. For imitation is merely a copy, just an approximation. "Mimicry" isn't the most faithful copy of the original. I can hear my son filing suit against his sister from the back of the van: "Daddy, she's copying me!"

The saints are not perfect. In flimsy, clumsy ways, they embody Scripture. But their very failure gives glory to God, in the same way that our imperfect, failed preaching glorifies God.[10] Preachers, instead of scouring about for catchy illustrations that only tangentially illustrate the text, might be wise to study the lives of saints, the great saints of history but also those we actually preach to, and discern the ways in which they naively, flawlessly, and stunningly embody texts, and name their faithfulness as the literal enactment of a text. To do so may require a more intensive connection between the life of the parish and the preaching ministry, ties too feebly explored and little understood, but crucial for the truthfulness of preaching.

When Sermons Happen

8
Delivery

If there were ever a perfect word to describe the strange activity of preaching, it is "delivery." The sermon is *delivered*—not spoken or imparted or extemporized, but delivered. What else is delivered? The mail? Like the mail carrier, the preacher absolutely must show up—rain, sleet or snow—with a big bundle or just a few trashable bulk items, with ads to buy something useless or a chance to win millions, with nothing of interest or that one letter that reveals either dawning love or immense loss.

The preacher delivers, and the image is apt, since much of what we find in Scripture is quite literally mail—somebody else's mail, in fact. We have alluded to the way that Barbara Brown Taylor has divulged how she thinks of sermon delivery:

> When I preach sometimes I feel like Cyrano de Bergerac in the pulpit, passing messages between two would-be lovers who want to get together but do not know how. The words are my own, but I do not speak for myself. Down in the bushes with a congregation who have elected me to speak for them, I try to put their longing into words, addressing the holy vision that appears on the moonlit balcony above our heads. . . . As a preacher I am less a principal player than a go-between, a courier who serves both partners in this ancient courtship.[1]

Perhaps it is liberating, perhaps it eases some of the pressure, to realize that we merely deliver. The sermon isn't about me. It's something going on between them and God. I'm a courier, a letter-deliverer only.

Or a midwife. For millennia, midwives (understandably women) have *delivered* babies. They are neither mother nor child, but they are there, assisting, encouraging, actually the first to glimpse and hold new life, but handing it off, washing their hands as someone else's child is born. Helping new life to be born, being an agent of delivery, is subversive. The exodus from Egypt happened only because two midwives, Shiphrah and Puah (whose elegant names mean "beautiful" and "lovely flower"), mocked the might of Pharaoh, and Moses and other boys survived the genocide (Exod. 1:15–21). To bring a child to birth is like preaching. It is a defiant "No way!" to the meaningless cynicism of the world. It is a vote, even God's vote, that life is good, that there is a future, even for something as vulnerable as a child, as precious but imperiled as Jesus in the manger.

The real labor of delivery, though, isn't the midwife's, but the mother's. "Pangs" is a mild word to describe the piercing pain, the shrill ache, the wild struggle of childbirth. The delivery of the Word only seems less wrenching, for those who have climbed onto the birthing table called a pulpit know a trauma of the soul, a palpable agony, struggling to get the thing out, to issue some Word that might live and grow. Isn't the Word of God happening in the real world comparable? The night before he was crucified, Jesus spoke rather poignantly to his closest friends—and how far away was his own mother on that fateful night?

> Truly, truly, I say to you, you will weep and lament, but the world will rejoice; you will be sorrowful, but your sorrow will turn into joy. When a woman is in travail she has sorrow, because her hour has come; but when she is delivered of the child, she no longer remembers the anguish, for joy that a child is born into the world. So you have sorrow now, but I will see you again and your hearts will rejoice.
>
> (John 16:20–22)

Delivery of the Word is laborious, with attendant pains. The Word is never neat, squeaky clean and comprehensible. The Word always comes out messy. We do not know precisely what it will be, we are more clueless about its destiny, we wonder if all the fingers and toes will be there—although we know it will be fingers and toes, flesh and blood. The Word is life: "The Word became flesh and dwelt among us" (John 1:14). Therefore preaching is difficult but tangible, excruciating but delightful—and harder than we'd ever imagined.

Mothers preparing for such a miserable, wonderful day take classes, practice breathing techniques, and take a coach (sometimes a spouse but not always) along for the ride. We will say more about techniques and helpers, but—to stick with the mailman, midwife, and mother notions—let us mark the immense weight, the unspeakably enormous importance, of the peculiar talking that preaching is. All public speaking is notoriously challenging, and everyone with a pulse gets nervous when asked to stand up alone in front of people and say a few words.

YOU SHOULD BE NERVOUS

But preaching isn't a Toastmaster's speech on some topic, or a training course for the sales force. We are talking about God, life and death, salvation or perdition, morality or decadence, love or hollowness. Who else has to talk about such heavy subjects? The doctor who has called you in to explain whether the biopsy turned out to be benign or malignant? The parent, buckled by guilt, who must apologize to his children for a pattern of alcoholism and infidelity? The officer who shows up on a porch to say, "Your son was killed in action while serving his country"? The lover who protests her love for the beloved? Preaching, the delivery, the birthing of God's Word: the weight of the thing can crush the most muscular of us.

No wonder preachers get that deer-in-the-headlights look. No wonder we strike people as a tad rigid, anxious, or even wooden. Whether it is sheer personality weirdness, or a realization of the gargantuan responsibility we bear, something unnatural creeps into the preacher's body and soul. We become possessed by some sort of artificiality, a numbing fear. Some paralysis of the inner self protrudes through the skin, exudes through the eyes. A sermon, devised to deliver a life-giving Word from the Lord, sags under its own weight, and the drag of a sense of inability tumbles the preacher with the congregation in tow down with a silent thud.

Before sermon delivery is a technique, it is a wrestling with the self. Technique will never matter until we gravitate toward some resolution of the self, some embrace of who I am, who God is, what's rattling around inside me, and how we can give birth to a child or show up with some wanted mail despite everything. Every preacher, just like every Christian out there who listens to preachers, suffers some degree of inner turmoil, a discomfort beneath the skin. Don't bleed out during the sermon, but between sermons go to that dark place and work on issues. Trust in the principle Rilke wrote about to a younger friend:

> Do not believe that he who seeks to comfort you lives untroubled among the simple and quiet words that sometimes do you good. His life has much difficulty and sadness. . . . Were it otherwise he would never have been able to find those words.[2]

Believe that God works, not through our abilities, but through our inabilities, our disabilities, even our craziness. "For my power is made perfect in weakness" (2 Cor. 12:9). Your inner weirdness will peek out during the sermon, or poison the preparation process. Your dis-ease within will creep onto the surface of your face and possess your body parts, betraying a wonderfully conceived sermon. Work on whatever riddles your soul, but then trust the way God can actually deploy your flawedness for the benefit of flawed people with riddled souls.

Don't let nervousness loom as your foe. You *should* be terribly nervous. If you lose an edgy unease about preaching, you should sell insurance or retire. Nervousness can be a valued ally. A nervous sweat might expose a lack of confidence, but then again it might be a visible clue that we are talking about something that matters, really matters, that can't be messed up but just might anyway, because it's too large, too much is at stake, and I'm not up to this. The very exhibition and then perception of nervousness oddly underline the marvel of the preaching moment.

NOTHING TO HIDE

The ultimate goal in sermon delivery isn't to mimic some great orator, but to be yourself. Most sermons I witness that falter are shipwrecked on the rocks of artificiality, the hell of pretending to be somebody else, the masking of the truly fascinating person God made the preacher to be. Some preachers seem quite boring in their delivery. But I have never met a boring person. Every person (and preachers are persons before and while they are preachers) is chock-full of quirks, humorous moments, thrilling and heartbreaking memories, with identifiable facial expressions and vocal intonations, each as unique as a snowflake. Every preacher is an intriguing person. Trust your inner intrigue, your peculiar charm. Throw off the shackles of fakeness, and quite simply be yourself, be natural, be the one God made once upon a time.

Self-consciousness is a killer in preaching. But to shed self-consciousness, you need to become conscious of your self and how you beam your self out to the world. Mirrors can be helpful. Winston Churchill never spoke before Parliament without having seen his own talk in advance—in the mirror—as biographer William Manchester humorously narrates:

> When delivering a major speech, Churchill came armed with everything he was going to say, including the pauses and the pretended fumbling for the right phrase. Many of his speeches were written in the bathtub. One of his valets was surprised on his first day to hear his master's voice rumbling from the bathroom. He put his head in and asked: "Do you want me?" Churchill rumbled, "I wasn't talking to you. I was addressing the house of commons." Each speech was typed in "psalm form." He practiced endlessly in front of mirrors, and often in the nude. . . . One day he was visiting in the White House. Roosevelt wheeled his chair into the room, was surprised, apologized, and turned to go—but Churchill held up a detaining hand, saying solemnly: "The Prime Minister of Great Britain has nothing to hide from the President of the United States."[3]

First, the mirrors—and perhaps with clothing on. Actually DVDs of your preaching will help (not CDs, which obscure the visual elements of the sermon), although they are after the fact. You can learn much once the sermon is done, especially if you watch with someone who loves you enough to tell you the truth. Mirrors allow you to see yourself in advance. I have never preached a full sermon in front of a mirror. But I have rehearsed the opening, a key moment, a strategic sentence, or a particular gesture I wanted to be just right. I may see I have bags under my eyes or that my hand looks a little stiff. So I relax, or try to get a good night's sleep. If I can look at myself preaching and bear it, harsh critic of myself that I am, then I become more confident of the people out there being able to bear with me.

More importantly, I get my hands, my eyebrows, my grimace or grin just right. Sometimes our bodies betray us. I once saw a man preaching lovely words on John 11. When he got to Jesus saying, "I am the resurrection and the life," his face and words were entirely appropriate to his superbly invitational comments on the matter. But, oddly, he held his hand in front of his body, balled up into a fist. People notice a fist in their faces. On review, he tried the gesture again—same words, same voice and face, but this time with an open, relaxed, uplifted palm: powerful, tender, evocative, no longer a conflicted, mixed message.

Mirrors and DVDs help us to see if we are stiff, if we are ourselves. Videotape a sermon; then keep the tape running, and watch yourself have a conversation with somebody as soon as it's over. You inevitably are more engaging and interesting in the conversation. Try to duplicate that manner, those gestures. One of my preaching students offered a sermon in which he had several pauses; the feel was that he was struggling, lost, trying to find his place on the paper. We who watched rooted for him, but it was hard to stay on track. Then we kept the camera on while the class conversed about his sermon. He paused, just as he did during the sermon, but it felt different. We felt he was thinking, probing his heart for the right word, and it was lovely.

Fast forward through a DVD of a sermon. You notice swaying or ridiculously repeated gestures in a way you don't in slow motion. Then vary whatever it is you are doing. Mirrors and DVDs help us see if we are stiff, or if we gesture—but gesture can become wild gesticulation. Can we get our words in sync with our gestures? Are we hanging on to the pulpit for dear life? A gesture can be more powerful than a word. The lifted eyebrow can evoke more wonder than lots of words about wonder. Ponder the gestures of others, and your own, in sermons and in routine conversation. Hans Georg-Gadamer was on to something shrewd when he wrote, "The whole being of a gesture lies in what it says. At the same time every gesture is also opaque in an enigmatic fashion. It is a mystery that holds back as much as it reveals."[4]

We fret too much over illustrations, forgetting that your body is itself illustrative. If you are speaking of repentance as turning, as making a 180-degree turn, then face your body one way and then the other. If the Gospel is that God did not remain aloof in heaven but came down, look up with an arm raised high, then glance down, lower your arm. If you are expostulating on the futility of the law, wag your finger to depict what the law tries to accomplish. If you are demolishing a bad idea, shake your head and sigh. But be natural. Be you. You are not stiff. In daily conversation you use your body in some way to express yourself. Be yourself in the pulpit—or even more of your self, daring to be your truest self as you literally embody the Gospel.

In one way, we learn all we can from great public speakers, drama coaches, or stellar actors, because preaching is a kind of acting. But at the same time, as you strive to improve the dramatic mode of your presentation, keep that BS detector on high alert. There must be a way to maximize voice, eyes, body, and gesture without becoming a fake, or manipulative.

Churchill practiced his pauses and fumblings. I know many preachers who mark up their manuscript with stage directions, like "long pause," "look quizzically to the ceiling," "stammer over this sentence." In social intercourse, not many of us speak smoothly, with flawless grammar, hatching long sentences with subordinate clauses. We get choppy; our sentences are incomplete, or our thoughts are in what Churchill called "psalm-form." Practice talking the way people talk, the way people hear. The smartest, most eloquent people I know pause, fumble, and say words that never appear in many manuscripts, like "Um," or "Gosh," or "Hmm." Michael Erard has written a wonderful book, perfectly titled: *Um . . . : Slips, Stumbles, and Verbal Blunders, and What They Mean.*[5] While many preachers blunder too much, and say "uh" or "ya know" far too many times, a pause, a stammer, a pregnant "oh, what shall I say next?" moment can leave some space for the listener to fill in the blanks, or even for the Holy Spirit to get a word in.

Theologically we have even better cause to stumble, fumble, meander, sigh, scrunch up our face, and stammer. Our subject matter isn't a brick or a peanut. We are talking about God. Preaching really is a "raid on the inarticulate."[6] In the presence of the holy God we fall silent and expose the laughable inadequacy of mere words. To stutter, to sound befuddled, to struggle and fail to find the words: I do not believe this confuses listeners as much as we might imagine. A blundering "um," a pause, a fumbled sentence may just usher listeners into the very heart of life before God. Even to brush the hem of God's garments, however briefly, should strike us all dumb. A sermon that is smooth, totally eloquent, and flawless in language and logic may just misrepresent the nature of God incarnate, who became quite human for our sakes.

MANUSCRIPTS AND MUSICAL NOTATIONS

So should I use a manuscript? Or notes? There is no easy answer to this sort of query. You have to find what works for you. Eye contact should, of course, be maximized, since preaching is something you do out loud with other people. The most beautiful moments in life are when someone looks at someone else deeply and utters words that matter. So the preacher's head simply cannot be buried in paper hidden on top of a pulpit. You may need paper, although you might gamble a little: run the immense risk of trying a few sermons without any paper at all. Paper can become your enemy. Invisible rubber bands pull your eyes downward, and you become a bobbing-head preacher. That's no way to say words that matter. If you must have paper, be intentional about when to look up and down, and don't even try to pretend the paper isn't there. Our tendency is to look down at the end of a thought packet. Why? You are fretting over "What's next?" But looking down at the close of a little clump of a message is like looking at your lover while you are saying, "You know, since we've been dating for six months now, I just wanted to say . . ."—and then looking away as you finish with, "I love you and want you to marry me." Your head has to be up for the clincher. Finish it. Look them right in the eye. Then, and only then, look down for what's next. You'll find it. If it takes a second or two, that's good for them, as they can let the thought you just shared with them eye-to-eye marinate.

If you must have paper, let it become a prop. Instead of masking the fact that you need paper, pick it up, let them see you holding it, even reading it if you need to. But look at the paper as if it is pure gold, as if it bears a stunning new discovery. Eudora Welty imagined a couple who, as they grew older, read to one another: it was "the breath of life flowing between them, and the words of the moment riding on it that held them in delight. Between some two people every word is beautiful."[7]

If you must have paper, equip the paper with more than the words you plan to say. Mark it up with squiggly lines, arrows, facial expressions, stage directions. If you are unsure how to do this, talk to someone who teaches drama. Circle a phrase and notate: "Use low, growling tone." "Chuckle when you say this." "Grimace and glance to the left." Preaching is drama. You are delivering new life, and nobody keeps a straight face or speaks in straight, dull tones in the delivery room. You are in pain, so you raise your voice, shiver, groan, laugh, whisper. Plan on it; prepare to embody the giving birth that a sermon is.

Every sound that comes out of your mouth has a pitch you could plot on a musical staff. Investigate the range and the "melody" of your sentences. Say a word, then elongate it: it's an F-sharp! What pitch is the next word? What is the melody of a sentence? Far too many preachers get into a singsongy pattern that looks like this:

A few beats gradually bumping up the scale, then cascading back down. Listen to gregarious conversations among people or to great actors. They do not use this lilting up-and-down chatter very often at all. This singsongy pattern becomes dull, and has a sugary, sappy feel. So the musical notes of your talking betray you, and the sermon feels trite while you are trying to say something meaty. Attend to your tonality, finish a sentence going up. Or notice you are too up at the beginning; so where can you go? The whole sermon sounds shrill.

Measure how broadly your voice is being used. I know preachers who can sing a wide range of notes, but in preaching there is a constriction, a narrowing of deployed pitches. Practice going higher, and lower; expand your range; be intentional about exploiting the voice God gave you.

Musical notes are not all. There is volume, and intensity of voice. Sometimes preachers get really intense vocally about something that is of no consequence. Save it for the punch line, the utterly pivotal declaration. What about pace? Many of us talk too fast. But fast talk can express perfectly what you are trying to say. I heard a friend one time explaining from the pulpit the frantic pace of life in America, how we never are still before God. He got faster and faster, louder and louder, tumbling frenetically through his catenation of all we do to stay so busy. Then suddenly he halted, took a long breath, and said slowly, barely above a whisper, "God said, 'Be still, and know that I am God.'" The words on the page were about being busy and our need to be still; but even if you spoke no English at all, you could have understood what he was about simply by observing his tone, pace, and volume, as vocally he embodied and illustrated the very contrast he was talking about.

Watch comedians who impersonate famous people. Impersonations can be of immense value in preaching. You don't pretend you are Abraham or Judas or Miriam. But if you are speaking of anger, sound angry. If you are talking about the vapid empty-headedness of our culture, don't sound wise; speak empty-headedly, with a silly tone. If the world says, "Hey, go for the money," use a seductive tone to capture the seductiveness of our culture.

Silence may be a great friend in preaching. Allow for pauses. Let them linger; be comfortable with them. Gadamer has written,

> When we say that someone is struck dumb or speechless, we do not simply mean that he has ceased to speak. When we are at a loss for words in this way, what we want to say is actually brought especially close to us as something for which we have to seek new words.[8]

Trust silence. God is a friend of silence, and it can be the still point where the Spirit rescues your sermon from being simply too many words.

SHEDDING LOVE

In some ways, the most expressive but vulnerable member of the body must be the face. You probably have a handsome face, or you may not think you do. The face is essential in preaching, and an attentiveness to the face and what it is conveying can clinch or ruin a sermon. It may be helpful to practice in front of a mirror and check out what your face is actually doing. A self-consciousness about the face will tip off people watching that you are somehow ill at ease in your skin. Just be. Know the grace of God, and believe it. Get centered in who you are. Trust God. Love the people, and feel considerable compassion for them. Your face will embody this calm, and the less anxious you are, the more your face will be a transparent window into the heart of God. Your self peeks out, and you will never do better than simply to be yourself, to let the person God made you to be simply happen in the pulpit.

My ideal, my lifetime goal, is to be like a preacher marvelously portrayed by George Eliot. In an unforgettable, shimmering scene in *Adam Bede*, the folk from town have learned of a Methodist preacher coming—and a woman at that. Her message is simple, unaffected, compelling, and Eliot sets up the sermon itself with a portrayal of Dinah and her physical bearing:

> Onlookers had known but two types of Methodist—the ecstatic and the bilious. But Dinah walked as simply as if she were going to the market, and seemed as unconscious of her outward appearance as a little boy, no attitude of the arms that said "But you must think of me as a saint." There was no keenness in the eyes; they seemed rather to be shedding love than making observations. The eyes had

no peculiar beauty, beyond that of expression; they looked so simple, so candid, so gravely loving, that no accusing scowl, no light sneer could help melting away before their glance.[9]

Dinah's sermon itself is a masterpiece, one preachers should study and emulate, an example of simple yet well-chosen words straightly presented that common folk will not only comprehend but also find mesmerizing.

> The simple things she said seemed like novelties, as a melody strikes us with a new feeling when we hear it sung by the pure voice of a boyish chorister; the quiet depth of conviction with which she spoke seemed in itself an evidence for the truth of her message. She spoke slowly. . . . The effect of her speech was produced entirely by the inflections of her voice, and when she came to the question, "Will God take care of us when we die?" she uttered it in such a tone of plaintive appeal that the tears came into some of the hardest eyes. She was not preaching as she heard others preach, but speaking directly from her own emotions and under the inspiration of her own simple faith.

Eliot's picturesque telling of "The Preaching" reaches its zenith when various listeners are deeply moved, as she puts it, for "there is this sort of fascination in all sincere unpremeditated eloquence." Are your eyes making observations, or shedding love? When you process into the sanctuary, do you seem to be walking to the market, or to the guillotine?

Above all else, once you have explored these counsels and others you'll read or stumble upon, find yourself. Everyone who has ever been brilliant, or even pedestrian, is the sum total of various influences. Exploit that, then move on, perhaps in the way one biographer described Mozart:

> At a certain point in his development, a gifted young composer becomes more than the sum of the influences he has absorbed from tradition, more than a transmitter of conventions. He becomes an adept, he speaks in a tongue that has not previously been heard, he finds his voice. He has discovered a style; or, perhaps, a style has discovered him. . . . Mozart was indeed a master imitator, capable of working in a large variety of styles.[10]

Mimic others, stretch; but then find your own voice, live into your own body, let your face be the face of the Gospel. Then, when you are done, consider what is next. You are not nearly done with your sermon.

9

Aftermath

During my first year or two of preaching, I read Frederick Buechner's impressionistic thoughts on what happens at the very beginning of the sermon, or right before the beginning, when the people have sat and fallen silent.

> The preacher climbs the steps to the pulpit with his sermon in his hand. He hikes his black robe up at the knee so he will not trip over it on the way up. His mouth is a little dry. He feels as if he has swallowed an anchor. If it weren't for the honor of the thing, he would just as soon be somewhere else. . . . The preacher pulls the little cord that turns on the lectern light and deals out his note cards like a riverboat gambler. The stakes have never been higher. Two minutes from now he may have lost his listeners completely to their own thoughts, but at this minute he has them in the palm of his hand. The silence in the shabby church is deafening because everybody is listening to it.[1]

I tried to live into that moment. I would climb (notice we use the verb "climb," and I tried to feel the arduous quest for the summit) into the pulpit, pause pregnantly, silently pray just a sigh to God, then look up, my eyebrow slightly creased, and utter some weighty sentence.

But my moment seemed to be mine alone. When I looked at the people—not when I beamed my beatific gaze at them, but when I really looked at them—I realized they were not quite ready. Dad was handing crayons to Junior, who had just dropped his "little worshiper" bag. A woman put on her sweater. The card in the hymnal rack suddenly caught his attention, and the woman next to him remembered she hadn't silenced her cell phone. Even when I talked and they were listening (and this may just have been me), it seemed to take them a minute or two or four to adjust to me, my cadence, my face; out of a whizzing world of rushing about, and now out of a worship service of fairly continual activity, the people had to sit, listen, and frankly do some work in thought, reflection, and conversation (albeit silent dialogue, at least where I preach). They were not yet in the palm of my hand (and I add the "yet" quite optimistically, knowing many Sundays they eluded my grasp).

I am far more interested in the last moment of the sermon than the first. When it's over, you say, "Amen," or close your eyes to pray—or perhaps to avoid eye contact with the people to whom you just spoke. How did it go? It can feel like *American Idol,* and you sense votes are being cast. Good sermon! Man, he missed two good stopping points. I don't agree with her, and don't like it when she talks politics. What do you want for lunch?

They may be having the preacher for lunch. The people didn't go to seminary and learn that worship is something the people offer to God. They come as moviegoers or theater critics, and they do not mind dicing up the day's sermon—even for the clergy they love and adore. His sermons are okay, maybe a little boring at times, but he's such a good pastor. Thud.

My suspicion, though, is we are probably far harder on ourselves than the people out there are on us. They are quite accustomed to trite, silly, thin, boring fare (hence the popularity of lame television programs and the success of absurd advertising). So if you say anything that matters, and happens to be simultaneously true, you have probably done them a tremendous favor. But we do ourselves no such favors. Do the people have the preacher for lunch? Or do we chew up our own egos? The Austrian novelist Heimito von Doderer was sadly correct: "In comparison to what I've suffered from myself, the humiliation and suffering inflicted on me by others vanishes into insignificance."[2]

I believe this "aftermath," the way we evaluate ourselves, second-guess what we said or didn't say, or simply bemoan our inability to get a good message across, has a crippling effect over time. We grind up what we just preached, and maybe it lingers past dinner and we toss and turn a night or two. Perhaps somebody grinds up what you just preached, with some sweet advice, like "Have you thought about preaching on self-esteem?" or "Why didn't you honor our veterans?" or "Here's a sermon from a guy I heard at my daughter's Church last Sunday; he was fantastic." Or a committee charged with the congregation's welfare musters their courage and has a sit-down to ask you to try to preach more briefly and to inject some humor. Or maybe they just want a new preacher, period.

The aftermath does not merely poison your memory of last week's sermon. It jades how you prepare for the next one. You feel stuck in whatever your pattern might be, and you're sure it's not a pleasing pattern. Or you are down in the dumps, and in such a mood you just can't think up anything hopeful to say. Or twenty-seven people adored your sermon, but one guy dashing off a critical e-mail sticks in your craw, and he is sitting in your lap when you try to incubate the next one. A season of negativity, a lifetime of harsh self-reviews, can devour the heart.

I suppose there are preachers who take a sunny view of what they just preached, feel a bit optimistic about the results, and strut a little—and this too can have deleterious effects that are harder to contemplate. But, on the whole, the human nature we may characterize accurately in a sermon—our fallen nature, our tendencies toward frustration, our habit of focusing on the negative, our outright fear of failure—is precisely what dogs the preacher when we look retrospectively at a given sermon or a lifetime of homiletical effort.

FAILING TO STRIKE FIRE

The aftermath does not always wait until the sermon is over and you have sat down. Mid-sermon, you begin to feel the reviews. You try eye contact, but the first guy you engage has a blank gaze, politely pointed in your direction. Or a puzzled look indicates that the logic you so relished just last night is eluding them. They're shuffling in their seats . . . and there is the fourth or fifth person who can't wait five more minutes to go to the bathroom. What is she hunting in her purse? And that guy in row seven who has nodded off is about to bang his head on the pew in front of him. You realize mid-sermon that it just isn't working. You didn't prepare as well as you could have or should have. Moldy images of a schoolteacher bloodying your paper with a C-, or a parent scolding you with some prophecy that you better work harder or you won't amount to much, are echoing through your cranium. Richard Lischer narrates one of his early efforts in the pulpit:

> It took the people of Shiloh about thirty seconds to recognize a preacher in trouble. An old woman in the second row said softly, Help him, Jesus. The entire congregation was witnessing the painful spectacle of a careful young man failing to strike fire.[3]

I know the feeling too well: failure to ignite. Or it burned a little, but too briefly to warm up the room.

So next time . . . and there is always a next time! It's not like golf: you take a few lessons, you keep teeing off into the woods, and you can just quit. You can't quit preaching. Sunday is coming, you didn't strike fire last week or the week before, and it seems increasingly unlikely anything will ignite this coming week. Perhaps you read something that rejuvenates, or you go to a workshop and hear somebody with a creative angle, or you simply are buoyant, and you feel a bit like Quentin, the lawyer in Arthur Miller's *After the Fall*, who battled much anxiety but optimistically declared, "Every morning when I awake I'm full of hope, I'm like a boy! For an instant, there's some unformed promise in the air. If I could corner that hope . . . and make it mine."[4]

There is hope for preaching, but the hope is not that we will finally master the skill and become so adept that we will attract a great nickname, the way St. John Chrysostom did. Chrysostom: "golden mouth." How lovely would that be? How ridiculously unattainable! And let me underline that the unattainability of a "golden mouth" reputation is good, God's surprising gift to us. We fail to strike fire, and yet we can figure out a way to stop the self-flagellation and discover ways to handle the inevitable critique that rises up from the people, and let the grace flow over the preaching enterprise.

Martin Luther took a typical, simple approach that, for me at least, feels too distant to embrace. For him,

> Preaching is as fully the Word of God as the incarnate Lord and the written Scripture. Therefore, any preacher who has finished a sermon should not pray for the forgiveness of its deficiencies, but should rather say "In this sermon I have been an apostle and a prophet of Jesus Christ." Anyone who cannot boast like that should give up preaching, "for it is God's Word and not (the preacher's) and God ought not and cannot forgive it, but only confirm, praise, and crown it."[5]

We do need some mental habits to help us to refrain from too much apologizing. For a few years, my father-in-law, himself a faithful preacher, would call me on Sunday afternoon and ask how the sermon went. I devised various answers: "Hundreds were saved." "The dead were raised." "Bryan got in a good nap, which must have helped him." Two of my jocular answers were probably the best. "I did my best." Probably I didn't. My best would have required a bit more study and practice. "I said true things." At some point we have to live with the sermon and be able to accept that, given the vagaries of the week and my own weariness and weakness, "I did my best," and "I said true things."

THE POWER OF AUDIENCE

Where do we find ourselves on the homiletical battlefield when it's over and we assess what transpired? We begin by acknowledging the audience's power over us. To deny their power is to deny that they exist or that preaching matters. Audiences have always held immense sway over speakers, and it may be more pleasant in our day than in ancient times. Dio Chrysostom wrote,

> The audience might cheer and applaud with enthusiasm, or raise an uproar, shouting the speaker down; they might sit, silent and indulgent, or pelt the speaker with stones out of rage; the mighty listen raptly in awe, or respond with jeering, hissing, derisive laughter or crude jokes. In short, the audience had it in its power to terrify and dominate the speaker if it cared to.[6]

Only on the surface should we feel bugged by this. Every relationship that matters works this way. My wife has the power to terrify or dominate or cheer or sit indulgently or be rapt in awe when in my presence. My children have the power to terrify or jeer or respond enthusiastically when around me. My friends have power over me. We call this *love*: you let somebody else have power over you. Preaching is love, and if the people matter, they wield a kind of power over you. Own it, get over it, and let life be birthed through the inevitable pain.

How else do we preach but then not come undone in the aftermath? Joseph Sittler once said:

> I can only teach in such a way as to engender in him the questions, as if he were saying to himself, "If it were true, it's a big enough

truth that would pull me together." In a sense, that's what a sermon is for: to hang the holy possible in front of the mind of the listeners and lead them to that wonderful moment when they say "If it were true, it would do." To pass from that to belief is the work of the Holy Spirit.[7]

To speak of the work of the Holy Spirit, "to preach and then trust the Spirit with the results," just seems too results-oriented, and doesn't help me reckon with my nagging inability to engender questions, to hang that holy possible before them. Or it feels like a flimsy cover for what may have been a pedestrian effort, or even for an admirable sermon that people fawn over but is not exactly the Gospel itself. And yet what was said of John Calvin feels true to me:

> A man whose holy life is given up to the service of God may preach irreproachably scriptural doctrine, applied with a profound psychological insight to the needs of the congregation, and yet nevertheless it cannot be taken for granted that God is speaking to His Church. Rather, Calvin would say, preaching *becomes* Revelation by God adding to it His Holy Spirit.[8]

More bawdy, but delightful, is the remark Luther made when asked how the Reformation happened:

> While I have been sleeping, or drinking Wittenburg beer with my friend Philip and with Amsdorf, it is the word that has done great things. . . . I have done nothing; the word has done and achieved everything.[9]

There is something to this, despite my hesitations. Sermons I am pessimistic about seem to do some surprising good, and sermons I deem quite polished and shrewd fall on deaf ears. It is humbling, and wonderfully liberating, to recognize that the Word isn't dependent entirely on me, can happen without me and despite me.

NICE SERMON

For a long time I tried to calculate the value of parishioner responses at the exit door. I have come to take pity on them, as they generally have no clue what to say. It is impossible to gauge the flaky but frequent

"Nice sermon" or "I enjoyed your sermon." Nice? Enjoyed? You were supposed to squirm, or give all your worldly belongings to the poor! Of course, many congregations have been told by some preacher that it is vapid to say, "Nice sermon," or "I enjoyed your sermon," so they refrain from a compliment—although in truth it's not the worst thing to be paid any sort of compliment.

Praise can, insidiously enough, be far more harmful than criticism. We begin to believe our reviews and to think, "I'm good in the pulpit! They love me! I should take this show on the road!" How do we receive any sort of review, positive assessments, negative critique, or, worst of all, the shout of silence? Praise of your sermon may frustrate you, but perhaps it is an unwitting way for the Christian to praise God. You need some praise, and the Church gives it—and the Church should give it. Isn't it good for the Church to be a band of encouragers? Take the praise for what it is: a garbled locution of belief sustained, of faith stirred, God made real in your talking; and they cannot think of anything else to say except "I enjoyed your sermon." Thanks be to God.

Young clergy face a daunting peculiarity in the aftermath. Early on, every sermon feels like a final exam in seminary or a referendum on "Should I really have gone into the ministry?" If the people are positive and encouraging in their reviews, are they simply taking pity on you as one so young, a fledgling colt being fed carrots in hopes of a better future? Be very clear: the young clergy suffer a debilitating disadvantage. Suppose you craft a prophetic sermon that should nail people's sinfulness to the wall, that challenges conventional thinking and lifts up the radical demand of the Gospel. The people have developed a clever defense mechanism: they nod, grin, and smirk a little, saying, "Ah, youthful idealism. I like it when the young clergy are so full of passion"—and you, but more importantly your message, is smoothly dismissed. There's no escaping it, unless you dare to name not only your own youthfulness but also the good company in which you find yourself: Jeremiah was a youth, and Jesus never preached past the age of thirty. Don't get too annoyed by the Church's sweet supportiveness of the young. Shouldn't the Church encourage those who are young? That they come, even pretend to pay attention, and then salute you for your passion is evidence of the hidden good in their hearts that there is hope for the Church, that there is still somebody who is young, and good, who has some passion for the Gospel.

Anyone who has preached much at all knows that some remarks made at the door or later in the week can be withering, a cruel lambasting, or just a bitter remonstrance exploding what you had thought was a fine homiletical offering. Sometimes you may get blasted, and frankly you deserve worse. In every case, we have only two choices: be devastated by the harangue, or accept it for what it is, learn from it, and move on. A pastoral heart is useful: how often is an explosion not really about the preacher or the sermon but a pent-up cry for help? An eruption, however hurtful, can often be a window thrown open into the new air of healing—if you can be the nonanxious presence and still love the one who seems to harbor so little love for you.

The reviews that tumble in can be indicative of the spiritual malaise in our culture, not anything proper to this individual congregation or you as an individual preacher. In my career, a dramatic shift happened when I wasn't looking. In my early days, if someone wanted to pay me the highest compliment conceivable, the parishioner would look me in the eye, shake his head appreciatively, and say, "Preacher, you stepped on my toes today." Now, no one ever says such a thing, and toe stepping elicits some kickback. Today, if someone decides to pay me the greatest compliment in their arsenal, she says, "Preacher, I agree with what you said." Our culture has moved a few thousand light-years in a direction that is perilous, for people are so insecure or close minded that they look to the Church to buttress their half-baked thinking, do not expect correction for malfeasance, and do not welcome the surgical procedure that preaching simply must be. Every person responding to your sermon lives most of their life outside the Church, drinking deeply from the well of a small-minded, fear-driven culture, and when you open the Church doors, all that garbage comes in with the tide. So it is not easy to know when a response is the kind of response a lover genuinely offers in the give-and-take of trying to figure out God, and when it is just more knee-jerk mirroring of our media-saturated, self-indulgent society.

Perhaps it is a good idea to raise the question for your people of what a sermon really is, what to listen for, what the risky allure of some preaching might be. In all of my parishes I have offered a class I tongue-in-cheek call "How to Listen to Sermons." People come, we have a good time together, but mostly we all walk away agreeing it is too trivial to waste our time gauging sermons by how droll they might be, or whether they had a catchy joke or anecdote.

SOME THINGS ARE BEST LEFT UNSAID

Supposing you are, though, in the name of the Gospel, getting through, making progress, chipping away at the edifice that is the world. Someone looks visibly moved by the sermon, and says, "Wow, that was really meaningful. I loved the sermon, it really spoke to me." You may be tempted to ask, "What about it spoke to you?" This sort of follow-up can be constructive, but it also can be humiliating. I have had people respond by saying, "Uh, well I can't really remember anything in particular, but it was something!" Years ago this bugged me, but not anymore. In a way, a sermon can be an experience in which someone, even the whole Body, is ushered into the presence of God, and you don't remember this or that point that was made, any more than you leave the symphony and say, "Gosh, when the oboe hit that F-sharp I was stunned."

When I have asked for more follow-up, I have also had people say, "I think your best thought was when you said . . ." Then they quote something I didn't say, or don't think I said, or something I would prefer not to have said. *C'est la vie.* I have also discovered that quite a few people do not really stick with me through the whole sermon. About one-third of the way through, I say something that so provokes a listener in the fifth row that she drifts away from the rest of my sermon and thinks, reflects, prays, rethinks. While I prepared a tightly argued case throughout the sermon, I think God does God's best work with such a sermon when my logic is simply ignored, and a single shimmering word launches someone into a new course.

In fact, a sermon just might achieve something extraordinary precisely when the listeners do not exactly understand the logic, the grammar of what is in the manuscript, or when the preacher is floundering about, not making much sense at all. In the film version of Stephen King's story, "Rita Hayworth and Shawshank Redemption," Andy Dufresne breaks into the prison's communication office with a 33-rpm record in hand. After shifting the loudspeaker microphone next to a phonograph, he lifts the needle and places it down gently. The stunned prisoners across the yard hear, first Susanna, then Contessa, singing "Che soave zeffiretto" (from Mozart's *The Marriage of Figaro*). Red marvels, and we overhear his thoughts:

I have no idea to this day what those two Italian ladies were singing about. Truth is, I don't wanna know. Some things are best left

unsaid. I like to think they were singing about something so beautiful it can't be expressed in words, and makes your heart ache because
of it. I tell you, those voices soared higher and farther than anybody
in a gray place dares to dream. It was like some beautiful bird flapped
into our drab little cage and made those walls dissolve away, and for
the briefest of moments, every last man at Shawshank felt free.[10]

We hope parishioners will leave church with some reasonable idea
what we have been talking about. But we must never forget that we
are talking in a gray place about something so beautiful it cannot be
expressed in words. What we leave unsaid may be the space for the
Holy Spirit to set people free. A sermon might have illogical moments,
while exhibiting a passion about Christ that might pick open the locks
on a few hearts. While the sermon is going on, listeners might overhear
something beyond the words, and believe rather hopefully that some
beauty lurks behind the words, above the ceiling, in the depths of the
heart.

But no matter how much we may improve our preaching skill or
how wisely we weather criticism or adulation, the lone crucial fact of
preaching, which we know viscerally and experience over the years of
hard experience, is that preaching quite simply fails. Why is this? Richard Lischer characterized the problem eloquently:

> The sermon, in fact, is Jesus trying to speak once again in his own
> community, but because he has assumed the full extent of our fal-
> libility, the power of his word is hidden and often disregarded by the
> world. . . . Preaching bears the impossible weight of its own message,
> which is God's willingness to be pushed out of the world and onto a
> cross. Preaching has to conjure with its own apparent irrelevance.[11]

How crazy is it to bother reading a book that tells you how to fail?
Theologically, no realization is more hopeful than this: we fail, and
our failure is the ultimate, underrated, and only meaningful goal of the
preaching enterprise.

10

Failure

Sermons fail. They all fail. Even the best sermon ever, from the best preacher ever, the one published in a book or on DVD that enthralls all preachers everywhere: every sermon fails—and at multiple levels.

Even the best sermon fails to capture the mystery, the grandeur, and sheer humility and mind-boggling grace of God. When it comes to finding the words to describe God, or even life with God, even the masters of words admit that they flounder. T. S. Eliot declares that he is groping for words, cognizant that each attempt is an ever-new failure, each venture "a raid on the inarticulate / with shabby equipment always deteriorating."[1] Shackled with such shabby equipment, we raid the inarticulate, not merely to describe God to our listeners, but to offer words up to God that are fitting—another impossibility. The ancient, eloquent hymn "O Sacred Head, Now Wounded" asks, "What language shall I borrow to thank thee, dearest friend?" We borrow, beg, steal words, trying them on for size, shaking our heads, trying again. The preacher's words tiptoe along a treacherous line, where words provoke, dare, strain, fail, wait, and try once more.

Even the best preacher fails, as people inevitably glue their admiration to the eloquence of the preacher and God is shielded from view, drowned out by the "Wow!" muttered by the crowd. Slick sermons fail; stupendous preaching fails by some paradox that makes us shudder. We strive to be as transparent as possible, to point to Christ, willing to stumble if needed, so that the viewpoint is fixed on Christ not us.

An old saying contrasts the two greatest orators of antiquity: When Cicero spoke, the crowds said, "What great rhetoric!" but when Demosthenes spoke, the crowds said, "Let us march." I have sought the "Let us march" type of response; but, as I think of it, I know who Demosthenes was, but I simply have no idea where or why he wanted the people to march.

I carry from childhood the memory of a stellar failure to speak of Christ. My sixth-grade Sunday school teacher was named Floyd Busby. He seemed to be at least 147 years old. He sported a flattop and spoke in a whiny voice. No one had bothered to train him in hands-on interactive instructional techniques that were age-appropriate. Why did he keep coming back Sunday after Sunday? We giggled and made fun of him behind his back—or at least we stupidly presumed to have cloaked our snickering.

But I remember Mr. Busby, and he changed my life. One Sunday, while we were yawning and poking at each other, he launched into a long, seemingly endless reading from his tattered Bible. We barely noticed the topic, the arrest of Jesus, how he was ridiculed, mocked, and beaten, how he bore a cross up a hill, how his feet and hands were nailed into the wood. Then, to our surprise, there was a long silence. No more of that whiny voice. We looked up from our silly games to see why he had stopped. His head was hanging down—and we wondered if he had died. But he wasn't dead. He was crying—and this was in the 1960s, when men just didn't cry. Somehow we resisted the powerful temptation to laugh. But the temptation subsided, for somehow we knew we were in the presence of something holy. He fought back his sorrow and said to us, "Don't you boys see what they did to my Lord?"

I will never forget Mr. Busby's love for his Lord. Because of him I can say "our" Lord. Years later, having gained a little maturity, and having been forever altered by the image of his plea, I tried to look him up and thank him for teaching me. But it was in vain. He was not to be found. He gave of himself all those years in teaching, probably with no compensation save the clamor of foolish, juvenile boys to get out of his room as quickly as possible.

BIBLICAL FAILURES

We know failure—and it is good. Karl Barth spoke of our inability to speak of God, and by our inability we give God the glory. When we are unable to preach well, or effectively—or whatever adverb we've been told is desirable—we are not alone. Moses said, "I am not eloquent . . . but I am slow of speech and of tongue" (Exod. 4:10). Paul did not apologize for his inability but boasted of it. Powerlessness was not just a theological datum he talked about; he exhibited powerlessness, proudly knowing that God's power is perfected not in superb homiletical expertise, but in weakness (2 Cor. 12:9).

Can we recall the vision of Isaiah in the temple? The sanctuary came to life before his very eyes, and the thrice-holy God spoke. Isaiah, dumbfounded, responded with words that immediately struck him as impoverished, even a bit unseemly: "Woe is me! For . . . I am a man of unclean lips." God healed his mouth, but this miracle did not set Isaiah off on a great career as an orator. At the precise moment Isaiah was commissioned to speak, God foreclosed on the possibility of success: "Go, say to this people, 'Hear and hear, but do not understand; see and see, but do not perceive.' Make the heart of this people fat, and their ears heavy, and shut their eyes; lest they see with their eyes, and hear with their ears, and understand with their hearts, and turn and be healed.'" No doubt dreading such a response to admittedly hard labor, Isaiah could only yelp in exasperation, "How long, O Lord?" (Isa. 6:5–11).

Alone among the biblical giants, Isaiah is linked to the preservation of words that fail but still matter. He responded to God, "Bind up the testimony, seal the teaching among my disciples. I will wait for the LORD, who is hiding his face . . . and I will hope in him" (Isa. 8:16–17). God charges those who speak on his behalf with doing precisely that. Once we have done so, and perhaps failed miserably, all that is left for us is to wait, not for success, but simply "for the LORD," our hope not that the sermon will eventually work, but only "in him."

Our inability to say what we are reaching after is a beautiful if not so eloquent testimony to the glory of God. The God of the Bible turns everything upside down and reveals the divine nature in the crucified body of Jesus. Jesus' broken body, his "failure," is precisely what infiltrates our words and liberates the message, revealing the hidden God. Our words are as vulnerable as Christ's body, but vulnerability is the stuff of beauty. Remember those beautiful moments, which are always riveted on important words being spoken and heard. When I say, "I love you," or "You really forgive me?" an embarrassing understatement has unfurled a beautiful, unanticipated world. Just think how much of Scripture is like this. The Psalmist cries, "My God, my God, why hast thou forsaken me?" (Ps. 22:1). A father pleads with his son to join the party for his younger brother. At Emmaus, the disciples' hearts burn within them. Hannah prays so intently that Eli believes her to be drunk. Breathless, some women stammer the news, "He is risen!" Inadequate words. Beautiful words.

FLAWED SACRIFICES

So offer your failure to God. All sacrifices are imperfect. In Old Testament times, even the best sheep carried to the altar was dirty and smelly. Our confidence is in the act of offering, or really in the one to whom we offer. Every offering fails: it is burned up, totally consumed, nothing substantial left, just some smoke rising. We dare not focus so much on so-called results, and if we are teased into doing so, we had best measure our desire by an astonishingly insightful letter Thomas Merton wrote to his friend and minister Jim Forest:

Dear Jim,
Do not depend on the hope of results. When you are doing the sort of work you have taken on . . . you may have to face the fact that your work will be apparently worthless and even achieve no result at all, if not perhaps results opposite to what you expect. As you get used to this idea, you start more and more to concentrate not on the results but on the value, the rightness, the truth of the work itself. And there too a great deal has to be gone through, as gradually you struggle less and less for an idea and more and more for specific people. The range tends to narrow down, but it gets much more real. In the end, it is the reality of personal relationships that saves everything.
You are fed up with words, and I don't blame you. I am nauseated by them sometimes. I am also, to tell the truth, nauseated by ideals and with causes. . . It is so easy to get engrossed with ideas and slogans and myths that in the end one is left holding the bag, empty, with no trace of meaning left in it. And then the temptation is to yell louder than ever in order to make the meaning be there again by magic.
The big results are not in your hands or mine, but they suddenly happen, and we can share in them; but there is no point in building our lives on this personal satisfaction, which may be denied us and which after all is not that important.

The next step in the process is for you to see that your own thinking about what you are doing is crucially important. You are probably striving to build yourself an identity in your work, out of your work and your witness. You are using it, so to speak, to protect yourself against nothingness, annihilation. That is not the right use of your work. All the good that you will do will come not from you but from the fact that you have allowed yourself, in the obedience of faith, to be used by God's love. Think of this more, and gradually you will be free from the need to prove yourself and you can be more open to the power that will work through you without your knowing it. . . If you can get free from the domination of causes and just serve Christ's truth, you will be able to do more and will be less crushed by the inevitable disappointment, frustration and confusion. . . . .

The real hope, then is not in something we think we can do but in God who is making something good out of it in some way we cannot see. If we can do His will, we will be helping in this process. But we will not necessarily know all about it beforehand.[2]

After all, a sermon is love, and love takes some peculiar delight in letting itself be wasted, squandered lavishly. The wise lover understands that effectiveness simply cannot measure love.

I cannot recall a more poignant preaching moment in a film than the one near the end of *A River Runs through It.* The father, who has lost his son to death, is preaching one of his last sermons before his own death. Without alluding to his son and their complex, puzzling, tragic relationship, he tells the truth about life, and about love, and his words make me think about preaching:

Each one of us here today will, at one time in our lives, look upon a loved one in need and ask the same question: We are willing, Lord, but what, if anything, is needed? For it is true that we can seldom help those closest to us. Either we don't know what part of ourselves to give, or more often than not, that part we have to give . . . is not wanted. And so it is those we live with and should know who elude us. . . . But we can still love them. . . . We can love—completely— even without complete understanding.

We love the Lord, we want to help the Lord, but we are a bit unsure what part of ourselves to give to the Lord. But we love. We may not understand. But we give a sermon, a valiant effort, certain to fall on deaf ears, yet somehow true in its fallibility, a holy offering to the God who asks only our willingness.

The Life of the Body

11

Preaching and Administration

"Oh, he's a good administrator." In ecclesiastical parlance, this may just be the kiss of death, code language for "Boring preacher, but he seems well-organized, sends a lot of memos, is solid on spreadsheets." We shudder at the prospect of ever being tagged with "Oh, he's a good administrator."

Clergy who conceive of themselves as more passionate about preaching—or the other theologically respectable tasks of pastoral care, missions, and education—too often view administration as drudgery, a hard necessity, labor that drains valuable time and energy, the price you have to pay to do the work you really want to do.

The gulf between our conceptions of preaching and administration seems as vast as the Grand Canyon. Administration feels like the business world, drab files of numbers, dollars, officers, forms, and policies, which loom menacingly as a grave peril to spiritual matters. We hold our breath and plunge into those murky waters of wedding policies and capital campaigns, juggling the politics of the place while trying not to drop the theological ball.

But this dichotomy between spirituality and administration, between true religion and organized religion, is a false one. Our error is theological in nature and exhausting in practice. Severing ministry into the spiritual and the administrative is the same as our dreadful habit of splintering apart the sacred and the secular. Nicholas Lash[1] suggests that as modern people we stand in the room of our selves, and there

121

seem to be two, and only two, windows into that room: the physical or tangible, apprehended by sensory perception, and the mental or spiritual, apprehended in varied but nonsensory ways. Spirituality comes and goes through the "mental" window or not at all. Spirituality gets cornered into bracketed zones, religious districts, distinct from seemingly worldly concerns like administration.

The Bible offers us a more robust view of the world. The Spirit of God roams everywhere. Nothing is "secular," all belongs to God, and nothing is finally alien to God's economy. A budget can breathe God's Spirit just as surely as a person at prayer. A policy on building use can echo the glory of God as profoundly as a theologically shrewd sermon. For years I underestimated the extent to which formation happens *outside* the official Christian education hour. We form (or malform) each other when we vote on building maintenance issues, when we wield the scalpel in a budget decision, when we converse in the hallway about a personnel matter.

Perhaps it is the peculiar responsibility of the pastor—and then of the leaders with whom the pastor has breakfast or coffee—to notice when something gets off pitch, and to "lead with questions" (as Jim Collins[2] wisely suggests). Does our retirement package say anything about who we are as the Body of Christ? Does our registration scheme for Vacation Bible School connect with the way Jesus welcomed outsiders? Does a facility-use fee glorify God or ostracize the one person we simply must reach? How might preaching undergird a revolution in administrative policy? And how might a policy realistically (and almost miraculously) undergird faithful preaching?

ORGANIZING RELIGION

When we hold administration in pious derision (even privately), we are succumbing to one of our society's most notorious mind-sets, the distaste of our era for "organized" religion. The world is full of spiritual people who are not fond of Church, almost as if the organizing of religion ruins it. But we are not saved or immersed in things spiritual so we might be alone with God. God's will is for us to be incorporated into the Body of Christ. Church is something we do together; and to come together and be the body of Christ, we must be organized. What could be worse than organized religion? Only one thing: disorganized religion.

Many preachers (many of whom became saints) of bygone generations were phenomenal organizers. We imagine St. Francis of Assisi in ecstatic rapture, or communing with doves and flowers, or preaching as if dancing; but he marshaled a throng of thousands who met regularly for meetings, adopted a rigorous order for personal devotion and public service, and became a force beyond Italy and into the whole world. John Wesley felt his heart "strangely warmed" and exited gilded pulpits to preach in the coal mines; but he also deployed hundreds of preachers on horseback across two continents, with systems of accountability, maps of regions to be evangelized, printed materials, budgets, and a hierarchy that would be the envy of the business world. Mother Teresa smiled warmly, prayed humbly, spoke eloquently, and cradled emaciated Indian children in her arms as a heroic example to us all; but she organized a new order of women who have enveloped the globe with a well-directed consistency that is a marvel of organization.

The world is God's, the institution is God's. So to be professional need not be at odds with being spiritual. Preaching is not a respite from administrative responsibilities. It is the heart of administration and requires its own very pragmatic administration. Money is not a necessary evil, but a gift to be incorporated into God's peculiar but beautiful economy. Money flirts with some insidious dangers and can poison the Body of Christ from within—if we get out of sync with our theology and cower before the rich, give them places of honor, and attend less zealously to the poor. Jesus did let the rich young ruler walk away, yet his preaching was absolutely on target about money.

We need to be intentional about how we discern and implement seamless continuities between a spiritual administration and the more obviously spiritual events of Church life, like preaching and the Eucharist. To paste a prayer on the beginning of a finance committee meeting will make no difference if we then carry on our budget deliberations as if we are not God's people, as if God's Word as not been heard, as if the teaching of Jesus and the cross and resurrection are fossils relegated to another room in the building.

We have witnessed discontinuity here too often. Once I preached what I thought was a compelling sermon on Luke 14, with sparkling observations on Jesus' admonition that "When you give a dinner or a banquet, do not invite your friends or your brothers or your kinsmen or rich neighbors. . . . But invite the poor, the maimed, the lame, the blind" (Luke 14:13). Then the education director stood up to proclaim that sign-ups for Vacation Bible School were beginning: "We'll sign up members' children first, then if there's room, nonmembers. We have to take care of our own!" Everyone who five minutes earlier seemed to appreciate my sermon now nodded approvingly at this seemingly self-evident announcement. The cow was out of the barn long before we thought about a possible engagement of Luke 14 with our Bible School registration policy.

Once I sat in on a congregation's local missions meeting; they were deciding what to do about a man who had been the object of much charity—failed charity in their minds—as this man quit jobs secured for him, resold groceries delivered to him and used the money to buy drugs, and worse. One man ventured a theological prop for why help to this "bum" should be discontinued: "We know the Bible says, 'God helps those who help themselves.'" Gracefully but firmly, an elderly woman replied, "No, that's in *Poor Richard's Alamanack*. The Bible says that while we were weak—not while we were trying hard, but while we were weak—Christ died for the ungodly."

Do our policies, our ways of ordering Church activities, our modes of conducting business in even feeble ways mirror the Gospel in which we believe, that we stand up and proclaim week to week? If we are attentive to this question, and if we learn to lead with loving questions instead of broadside swats at committee members, good things can happen. I had the good fortune of preaching on Ephesians 5 just a few days after our personnel committee charged us with devising a new hierarchical chart for our staff. While I was drawing boxes and arrows to diagram who answers to whom, who has the power and who doesn't, who reviews whom, I was laboring over these words: "Be subject to one another out of reverence for Christ" (Eph. 5:21). The dissonance was palpable. Then the following week I stumbled across a reminder of the way St. Francis organized his friars. Clearly he was the CEO, the hub of it all; he had the power of a simple word at which others would jump. But he structured things so that some random friar was placed above him, to whom he had to answer and be submissive.

As some of us conversed about this, we began to redraw our hierarchical chart. It became a seventeen-page document, but I think it is close to pitch-perfect theologically. One page describes the bulletin process, and the big cheese is Elaine, who types, edits, and prints the bulletin. For that process, I am her humble servant; she wields authority over me and the minister of music, and we are humbly accountable to get her information on time. The head of maintenance, on another page, is charged with caring for our facility; if he or his staff need you to shut down your computer or deal with the air being off for a while, you smile happily and ask when it is most convenient for them. Our pastoral-care minister is the grand pooh-bah when someone in the Church dies, and we all drop everything and ask him how we can be of assistance. In this scheme, everyone is submissive to somebody else, and the evaluations at year's end are written by quite a few people, and job performance is measured entirely by how well we submit to one another. Best of all, we are doing something that is theologically meaningful and not in conflict with the sermon preached on Ephesians 5:21, "Be subject to one another out of reverence for Christ."

Examples of this sort of interplay between preaching and administration could be multiplied endlessly, and every effort must be appropriate for the time, place, and circumstance of a given congregation. The key is the recognition that preaching and administration are not alien activities, but are like the palm and backside of a hand. If we detect a disconnect between what we preach and how we order congregational life and decision making, then we must laugh at our folly, sweep it aside, and begin again. How often in sermons do we speak of faith in God's power, but then hang our heads in committee with a sigh, chagrined that "We don't have the money" or "We could never pull that off"? Administration that is spiritually faithful rests in and zealously surges forward upon the Word of God, on the loving economy of Father, Son, and Holy Spirit, who never hang their heads or exclude children or bums.

TECHNIQUE AND LOVE

At the end of the day, the question will not be whether we succeeded, for we will have failed. Even the "Were we faithful?" question should humble the noblest of us, for we falter. We could also ask, "Did we love?" We can love, although all love falters as well. Yet in trying to sharpen our fidelity and our love, and to become excellent preacher-administrators, another fallacy dogs our thinking: ministry as "technique." In the name of doing Christ's work, we can trip headlong on modernity's insistence that every problem has a technological solution. We are mortal; but surely disease will yield to various surgeries and therapies. We struggle to rear our children; but proper methods of reading to them and investing for them will surely yield great adults. We feel isolated; but surely a menagerie of gadgets (mobile phone, iPad, etc.) will get us connected.

Sexuality has been entirely debased into a matter of technique. Instead of being the at-times clumsy but always heartfelt embodiment of tender love, vulnerability, and commitment, sex nowadays is expected to be gymnastic in nature: Is she good in bed? Does he delay my climax via some wizardry until the proper moment? Love is not a matter of technique, and our preaching and loving organization of the work of the Body of Christ never depend on getting our technique just right.

The proliferation of "how to" books cannot finally deliver on their promises, especially if we are lost or confused about where we are going. Thoreau was right about technological innovations: they generally are improved means to unimproved ends. The tasks of preaching and administration are not primarily matters of technique. There are techniques and skills to be learned, to be sure. We contemplate how business functions (or malfunctions) and pick up clues for how to handle meetings and personnel. Often Church structures were devised at least a full generation ago; while business and people have changed how things get done, the Church lags far behind, clinging nostalgically to outmoded decision-making processes. The Church has its business aspects, and we are wise to learn what there is to learn from computer geeks, planning consultants, and demographic strategists. We study actors, or the lawyers who frame their closing arguments so compellingly on television.

Technique will not usher in the kingdom of God, and the illusory promises of some church-management techniques and homiletical tips could in fact function as unwitting barriers to its dawning. There is no shortage of seminars and gurus who promise dramatic results, if we only go to this or that method of fund-raising or group dynamics or mass mailings. Seneca wrote that we are attracted to novelties rather than to great things, and Robert Frost delicately wrote "I gave up fire for form until I was cold."

Administration is the fire, the doing of great things; perhaps preaching provides the kindling, or the flint, the spark. What is required of the preacher-administrator is a posture of faithful expectation of that fire, or what Maggie Ross called "a willingness for whatever." We listen attentively to God's calling to us, to this congregation in this place. We weigh who is on hand, their abilities, histories, passions, goodwill, and we plot a strategy to get people out of the building to find the maimed, lame, and blind, to get the candles lit, to get shut-ins visited, to receive money to cover our operations and missions.

CULTURAL REVOLUTION

What generally is required is quite daunting: nothing less than a cultural revolution. When you arrive at a new congregation (a misnomer really, they are only new to you; they have been around for some time cultivating bad habits), it may not be pretty: worship is all entertainment with an incoherent liturgy, the small groups read all the wrong books, evangelism is nonexistent, mission is reduced to an annual car wash and barbecue sale, and the number one anxiety seems to be whether we will "meet the budget" (barely nudging out whether the new preacher will play golf like her predecessor).

Cultural revolution is required, even after you have been in a parish for four or fourteen years. Tares find their way into the heartiest field of wheat. Sin tugs at the heart of every church member individually and of the corporate Body of Christ. Even if a congregation excels, leaders and members become complacent and proud of past achievements. God constantly calls every Church—not just this one!—to the kind of intense self-scrutiny and radical change Jeremiah must have had in mind when he articulated his vocation as "to pluck up and to break down, . . . to build and to plant" (Jer. 1:10). As Marianne Williamson explained it,

> when you ask God into your life, you think God is going to come into your psychic house, look around, and see that you must need a new floor or better furniture, and that everything needs just a little cleaning—and so you go along for the first six months thinking how nice life is now that God is there. Then you look out the window one day and you see that there's a wrecking ball outside. It turns out that God actually thinks your whole foundation is shot and you're going to have to start over from scratch.[3]

As George MacDonald put it, instead of merely fixing the leaky roof, God knocks everything down but then adds a new wing, courtyards, and towers. "You thought you were going to be made into a decent little cottage; but God is building a palace. And God intends to come and live in it."[4]

A genuine revolution in culture requires more than stellar preaching, but it cannot happen without intentional preaching. I was taught that each sermon is a discrete entity, its value hinging on whether it is up to snuff exegetically and theologically. But every preacher needs a long-range strategy in preaching, and this is far more than simply plotting out texts and themes in advance. You are leading an organization. You have the bully pulpit, and in subtle, steady, and sure ways you paint a picture of what the life of the Body could be. About any text you could say quite a number of things, so why not say something about where the organization is heading, or dangle some images of where the organization might head?

This is a far cry from the kind of angry preaching that is little more than the venting of pastoral frustration, the withering critique that only crushes the soul of the Church. "There is therefore now no condemnation for those who are in Christ Jesus" (Rom. 8:1). Earlier we spoke of "ranking the subjects" and how the sermon is not a solo preacher speaking to a gaggle of solo listeners out there. We speak to the Body, and the response is not merely an individual response but a corporate reply—hands and feet, strong and weak parts of the Body rising up to act as Jesus in the world today. So we tantalize with stories of what it might look like when that Body is moving in sync with the Spirit, and we trust the beauty of the song (like that lyre of Orpheus) to keep the rowers moving forward together.

Cultural change—sadly, maddeningly, but wonderfully—happens slowly if at all. The preacher (in the pulpit but also in committee meetings, in conversations on the sidewalk, meeting with staff or leaders, praying, counseling, literally everywhere) must exhibit a focus, a true, pure vision, a patient calm. Ron Heifetz, writing about leadership in the business world, underlines the necessity of "pacing," recognizing that "the pains of change deserve respect."[5] So we learn to be urgent but in no hurry at all. "The Church is of God and will endure to the end of time." So the preacher must endure, while being the vehicle for the vision, without which the people indeed will perish, and trust that the Church really is of God.

CONNECTIONS

To consider this from a slightly different angle: the preacher-administrator has the best chance to fill the role we might call "patient representative." My best friend tried to find out why his aging mother's health was spiraling toward death; he discovered that she was seeing four different physicians for various ailments, each prescribing medicines, unaware of the work of the others. A few phone calls later they were connected, and a unified strategy restored his mother's mind and body to the land of the living.

Is the Church drifting into ever deeper confusion and flabbiness because we have compartmentalized church life? What if we got the preacher, the education people, the mission folks, the finance and building experts talking with each other and planning a concerted strategy so the church might actually be the Body of Christ, with the hands, feet, and other body parts working together with at least some semblance of agility?

I can't say when we stopped talking to each other and decided to dwell in not-very-splendid isolation. But when we do not work over-time on connections, we are contributing to the demise of the patient, the Church, the good people of God who yearn for meaningful link-ages between their Sunday School class, what the choir sings, the prayer chain, the in-home Bible study, the preacher's pontification, and how we make decisions about facility usage. If they cannot discern connec-tions within the church, how will they make those even more essential, life-giving connections between what goes on inside the Church and what goes on out there in the world on Tuesday morning or Saturday night?

If people speak of their Church "home" or of the Body as their Church "family," it falls to the preacher to be the godfather, the god-mother, who fosters this sense of family. Whether the church is large, small, or middling, everyone benefits and can be energized by coordi-nated planning, by a high-level vision to which everything everyone does is accountable; and it begins in faithful proclamation of the Word that is connected to the administration of the place. The work, in fact, becomes easier, is more productive, and requires not more meetings but simply smarter meetings. In the business world, companies are learning to move *From Good to Great* (as Jim Collins's book is titled): "When you have disciplined people, you don't need hierarchy. When you have disciplined thought, you don't need bureaucracy. When you have disciplined action, you don't need excessive controls."[6]

The highest compliment a worshiper can pay when exiting the service is not "Good sermon, preacher!" but, rather, "Hey, what you said in the sermon fit with that anthem the choir sang, and it was the very theme we discussed in Bible study Thursday night" (and then the worshiper's daughter chimes in with, "Look, I glued cotton and made a sheep—just like the one you talked about in your sermon"); or a trustee furrows his brow and suggests that the text might have some applicability to how the new parking lot is to be configured.

A kind of sloth can ruin the functioning of the Body; we cut corners and understandably take the easy way. But the easy way for the preacher isn't always the best way for the Body of Christ. The easy way for educators isn't always the best way for the Body. The easy way for musicians isn't always the best way for the Body. The cheap way for the finance committee is rarely best way for the Body. Perhaps we will never make much progress until we persuade church personnel committees to begin their evaluations by asking not, "How are you as an individual performing?" but, rather, "How is the team accomplishing their common purposes?" or "How have you grown this year in your ability to work closely with the rest of the staff and lay leadership?" Perhaps our nominations committees will need to ask not, "Are you willing to do this job? You're good with money, so oversee our money," but, "Do you understand what we're about as the Body of Christ? Can you guide this arm, this torso, this calf, this shoulder part of the Body to maximize what we are doing together?" Instead of assessing, "Does she preach good sermons?" they might analyze, "Is the preaching fostering a broad Church culture that is responding to God's call?"

ORGANIC PROCESSES

So the preacher begins to pay a little attention to what's going on in fourth grade Sunday school, or in week seven of a Bible study series, or what is theologically at the heart of a building-policy issue—and then during the sermon simply mentions something like, "We wonder what Moses thought when he saw that bush on fire," or selects for an illustration the way the decision to install an electronic door achieved accessibility and a family's life was fundamentally altered. People walk out of Church dazed, believing some bizarre coincidence has been orchestrated by the Holy Spirit—and they are not wrong to think so!

A few years ago, our pastoral care team was simply sharing out loud about what we had heard people struggling with in their lives. The biggest issue was "loneliness." So, instead of just shaking our heads and praying for the lonely, we suggested a Lenten focus on solitude—which is like being lonely, but so very different. We preached, we asked classes to think about loneliness and solitude, and our hospitality team geared up to insist that folks wear name tags and stay after worship for lemonade on the lawn.

People notice these things, and it matters. In *Good to Great*, Collins suggests that

> good-to-great transformations often look like dramatic, revolution-ary events to those observing from the outside, but they feel like organic, cumulative processes to people on the inside. No matter how dramatic the end result, the good-to-great transformations never happened in one fell swoop. Sustainable transformations fol-low a predictable pattern of buildup and breakthrough.[7]

So we begin to plan, to talk to each other, to draw ever more people into the circle, and make up our minds that, no matter how big or how small we are, we will do what we do together, and the preaching will be the glue that keeps us together. Whether the sermon is "good" or passes exegetical muster is irrelevant; each sermon is part of a larger preaching and administrative strategy to transform the Body of Christ. Conjure up in your mind the beauty of children holding hands, or any time you and somebody who mattered labored together hard, on some project or another. You may have stumbled or been less than fantastic in what you achieved. But you were together, you loved and labored, and the beauty in such company is the epitome of beauty on this earth. The preacher has the responsibility to imagine it and the privilege to speak of it, to ask for it, and to celebrate its dawning.

12

Preaching and Theological Formation

Among the connections the preacher hopes to make within the life of the Church, none should be more natural than with the educational program of the Church. Those who stand in the pulpit might actually be humbled to realize that significant, lasting change in people does not come from passive listening to talking heads, but in smaller groups. John Wesley's genius was that he preached but then pressed those who cared enough to respond into small cells or societies, where study, prayer, and accountability gave the faith a decent chance of taking root and becoming transformative.

Preaching that matters is keyed in to the educational program of the Church. Like a pincer movement, what happens in worship is woven in complementary ways with what happens in classes and groups—or at least in an ideal world it should be. My experience perhaps mirrors that of many pastors. When I exited seminary, I dreamed of being not just a good preacher but a "teaching pastor." Congregations under my care would learn sound theology and be shaped as faithful disciples. I would download my newly marshaled information on Scripture, doctrine, and practice into the brains and souls of parishioners. I would be Martin Luther writing catechisms for families in Wittenburg, or Karl Barth diligently instructing his confirmands in Safenwil, or Evelyn Underhill leading deeply spiritual retreats.

Although my career as teaching pastor has been punctuated by some surprises of grace, it has also been embarrassingly insipid at times. I can echo the lament of Gail Godwin's "Father Melancholy," Walter Gower: "My ministry has been a stop-gap one. I came along too late you see. The Church I wanted to serve started crumbling a long time ago. . . . Nobody gives a damn about symbols anymore, but they're the language in which we listen and speak to God."[1]

Christian formation in the parish has proven difficult for a thicket of reasons. Most people aren't coming to the Church asking to be formed, or re-formed. Their predominant hunger is for an experience. They want to feel better, and if I'm not careful, I put on my apothecary hat and dole out a few Jesus vitamins, pour a bit of spiritual caffeine, and get a substantial tip for my efforts. Virtually no one peers up at me in the pulpit, wondering which dogma I might clarify for them.

Many are looking for answers. These people want me to be the tech-help guy you phone when you can't get your spirituality to work quite right. Worst of all, the people out there who care about theological formation frequently feel they have already been formed, and they are checking me out to see if my theology is up to snuff.

Sunday school, which theoretically ought to be the bastion of theological formation, is typically banal. Children glue cotton onto construction paper and, "Voilà!" it's Jesus, the good Shepherd. Pleasant enough, except that adult classes don't seem to have matured beyond these little pastel lessons in triviality. In adult classes I overhear the sharing of society's biases. In my last parish we dubbed one class "The Young Republicans" and another "The Aging Liberals." What in modern-day Sunday School would be recognizable to Luther or Barth? What might my homiletical antidote be, given my limitation of fifteen minutes, to the hour the Republicans and Liberals just spent confirming one another's pet half-truths?

Mind you, people *do* need to feel better. They need answers, and many find meaning and a sense of belonging in Sunday School classes. Some formation does happen, despite the silliness of Church programming. I can never be sure if Church fails miserably at formation, or if it's happening at fantastic levels. Of course it's both. Maybe the simultaneous failure and success is a maddening sign of the kingdom of God: the failure being some kind of Barthian witness to the glory of God who stupefies even the most brilliant theologian, the success being a tiny nugget of hope the Spirit wafts into the mix to keep us getting up in the morning. Jesus did speak of a field with wheat and tares, so you can just let it all grow.

SIGNS OF HOPE

While I am bowled over by the theological ineptitude of the parish, I find myself in awe of the simple yet doggedly determined Christianity of many who sit before me each Sunday. The laity surprise me, if I give them the chance. I keep bumping into people whom I thought were totally malformed and discover that they know the Bible well, read it daily, have a sense of basic doctrine, and are offended if dogma is disrespected. They deduce wisdom from quite a few of my sermons that really were bumblers. They make me wonder: Do I read the Bible as well? Do the authors I admire, who strut through academic corridors, read it daily, and as humbly?

When I remember that the adventure is about the obedience of the Body of Christ, I see church members who take their vacation time to go to Latin America on building and medical teams, and I see volunteers serving soup every Tuesday. I continually learn about real disciples (some of whom I'm pretty sure were yawning through my last sermon) who put me in the shade when it comes to an embodied, generously orthodox faith. Someone culls their memory, retrieving some fine point I made four years ago.

The lessons from years of preaching, and trying to connect deeply with the educational program, are many. You can't download theology directly into people's brains from the pulpit. They think, they love, they question, they are reckoners. Amnesia tackles them week by week, so the formative process is far from cumulative. If I help them at all, it is by the tone I set, my own observable zeal for the material, and my trust that God is the agent of formation. The preacher creates nothing but the space where discipleship might happen if the Spirit blows.

Technology gives us cause to worry. Technology is not somehow inherently evil; but when my staff and I scramble to learn PowerPoint, snazz up the Web site, craft hands-on activities that involve everybody, the unspoken assumption is that theological formation will happen if we just get our technique right. But it's the love and the fumbling, awkward misstep that elicit mercy and tenderness—and a profound sense that love is happening precisely in the thick of faltering technique. Do parishioners look at me, at our staff, at the teachers, and think, "There is someone who loves—who loves me, who loves God"?

I never assume, and never belittle, what people know. Years ago I stopped including absurd assumptions in my sermons: "You'll recall what Ezekiel said." "We all grew up treasuring this hymn." "Of course

Jesus was raised from the dead." "Turn in your Bible to 1 John." I start from scratch. Here is a Bible. What is a Bible? Does it read like a novel? Well no, so how do we approach this thing? You have questions? Superb. Keep them flowing. You believe God shields good people from harm? Can you think of any exceptions? Of course you can. What is that about?

Can I be as patient as I want teachers and learners to be, as patient as God must be? I try multiple approaches, remembering that not all parishioners learn the same way. Preach differently week to week. Preach on something, then follow up with a class you might teach. Some folks out there pick up on e-mail or the Web, while others catch on in a class. Some like videos, while others are hungry for one-on-one moments with the pastor. Can I try this, try that, be willing to fail, then try something else?

While seminaries may not urge us to teach, or to become pastoral theologians, I believe that Church folk actually are waiting for their pastor to function as dean or theologian in residence. Preach sermons that are intentionally instructional and profoundly wedded to what is going on in the rest of the Church program. Gradually learn to flex a kind of veto power, thoughtfully exercised with restraint. Superficially cute but heretical curriculum items creep into Church life, and who else but the pastor can lovingly say, "There is a better, truer way. Try this"?

CONGREGATION-WIDE STUDIES

For all the good of the lectionary and denominational curricula, we have witnessed some astonishing marvels when we have engaged in significant, congregation-wide studies. One season during my first year at a new appointment, we studied the Apostles' Creed in depth.[2] The next year, we took four months and read Matthew. We had the little children reading Matthew and adults reading Matthew. Matthew was the devotional at the finance meeting, Matthew was the focus of house groups, Matthew appeared in e-mail boxes, Matthew was preached and sung. One staff member was a bit puzzled about this, and asked me in a planning meeting "But what is the desired outcome of this 'reading Matthew' time?" Trying to defuse her discomfort with humor, I replied, "Our goal in reading Matthew is that everybody will read Matthew." The reply settled around the room, and we decided that was exactly right. If an entire congregation reads Matthew together, good things will happen; the story of Jesus will have been read, closely, thoughtfully, with conversation, by the followers of Jesus. The fruits of the study were far greater, but we never attempted to program them in advance.

Let people read the Word together, and watch for what the Spirit will achieve that you could never have planned—and that could never have happened if we followed the usual run of lectionary hopping about the Bible, classes choosing their own curriculum, kids and adults on different paths, with paltry fare like a Q and A on "the empty nest syndrome" or a cobbled-together devotional or a bland conversation about "friendship."

Such congregation-wide studies require considerable planning and organization—and a willingness to forego what I might prefer on a given week, or to forsake the easy path. Musicians have to get serious about finding anthems and hymns to fit. But then the music program begins to get a glimpse of the way the music really emerges from Scripture and fits what's been happening in Sunday school. Committee chairs are even compelled to think about their business in the light of Scripture; if you are in a congregation-wide effort on Isaiah, you have to dig through there to find something for the opening devotional and prayer that fit the budget deliberation or the building policy.

Then the Church begins to look and feel like a body, a maturing, increasingly coordinated body, the Body of Christ, members interdependent on one another, making connections, discovering unanticipated strengths, plunging off in new directions together as a single unit, not hinging on this or that scintillating personality, or the hippest new book on the religious bestseller list, but on the Word of God, read and alive before Sunday comes, lingering throughout everything we do. Isn't this really what transpired in the earliest manifestations of Christianity? Followers gathered in a relatively large home, and somebody showed up to unfurl a scroll and read aloud a Gospel—like Matthew—in the hearing of everyone. They talked about it, they prayed about it, and then they went out into the stiff challenge of the world to put into practice what they had heard together. They didn't call it a "congregation-wide study." It was just what seemed normal for the Body of Christ.

Sometimes my parishioners laugh about the variety of subjects I am loony enough to stand up and teach. They witness the mirror image of my personal reading discipline, which might not work for everyone but has been splendid for my own private education. I plan a few months ahead to teach a class on something I know nothing about or want to know more about, or perhaps on a subject they want to learn about or should learn about. Then I nab a few books and am forced to read them and digest their contents so as to avoid embarrassment when the class rolls around. So those who show up get a one-hour introduction to the theological revolution of Martin Luther, or to the holy life of Mother Teresa, or to the peacemaking of Francis. Together we explore theological themes in film, or why bad things happen to good people. My preaching is enriched, and congregational life begins to hang together.

Teaching in concert with preaching compels me to attend to my own formation, which for the pastor only *begins* in seminary. I read what is orthodox, and regularly. I read theology that is "out of the box" and let the questions dispel my pet illusions. I avoid the how-to-be-an-effective-minister treatises that just might reshape me into a frightfully efficient and boring CEO. There is so much drivel in denominational bookstores.

A LARGER PERSPECTIVE

Perhaps I help best when I take the long view. Isn't it the pastor's job, after all, to help every teacher understand how today's lesson isn't just something to be endured, something you're "willing" to do? Isn't each lesson part of a lifelong theological education? Gluing cotton on construction paper is a piece in a quest to glue together a real education so that an adult in his sixties will have a sense of how Luke is different from John, and that the Pelagians who fill nearby churches really do have it wrong. You can deal with some spilled Kool-Aid if you know you're part of a bevy of educators shaping a budding lay theologian.

Admittedly, my efforts at theological formation feel futile at times, but it's my job, it's my vocation, and I have all the advantages on my side. The truth of the Gospel is truer than the fluff society serves up as gospel. Although it requires some fortitude to hang in there long enough to get people to thinking in more complex ways, the chiaroscuro of a deep faith is truer to life than the simplistic silliness of pleasant, flat-footed platitudes.

My quest isn't "theological correctness." At the end of the day, I want people to grasp the inner workings of salvation history, to understand the hiddenness of God in Christ, to grapple with the inevitable mystery that shrouds the Trinity, because the truth is beautiful, good, and helpful. It will win the day because it is strong enough to carry the freight, to answer the hard questions, to dispel illusion, to broker life.

Of course, failure is inevitable. My best work is feeble. After a lifetime striving for theological excellence within the congregation, the tares of bad theology still sprout up. People still lunge after the kookiest newfangled belief they heard over the watercooler. I try to remember that our task isn't to succeed famously, but to try humbly. At the end of my ministry, I want to be able to confess that while I was trotting people calmly around the track, I did make them a little nervous. I pray one day my daughter might echo the reassurance of Father Melancholy's daughter: "I believe in symbols, too, Daddy. . . . The results are still coming in."[3]

FAILURE IN FORMATION

Or not coming in. The gravest failing of ministry is that we too swiftly adopt worldly measures of "success." Was the money raised? Did the Sunday School run smoothly? Were people content and getting along well? Were more people brought into the parish? If preaching fails faithfully, our administration and formation efforts will embrace failure just as faithfully.

Jesus' first great story was about a sower who would be counted a fool or a failure. This sower flings seed everywhere—on the rocks, on the road, among the thorns—wasting plenty of seed; a clever, well-trained sower would focus more smartly only on the fertile soil. But the kingdom of God is profligate, spendthrift, more than willing to bear some failure, evidently desirous that the seed land every place or no place at all.

In Church life we need to embrace failure. The cross and the lives of the martyrs were not exactly success stories. Fear of failure is the ruin of ministry. The success story in ministry seems to be about the one who protects the Church's turf, pinches its pennies, keeps everything running smoothly and securely, and utters pleasant words. But if we follow the one who told us about the sower, we have to structure and order our congregational life and the sermons we preach for risk. Try ten things; if three work, that's three more than if we only tried one really supersafe idea. Celebrate goof-ups. Give an award every year for the most audacious idea that just didn't work out at all. Honor the staff member and committee of two who organized death-penalty vigils that were attended by the three of them and nobody else.

Our formation program and our administration, like preaching, revel in a calculus the world will never comprehend. Our biggest investment may need to be in a single soul, in a program that will touch only three people with AIDS, in a bold attempt to alter a city that falls flat on its face. We need never regret that we heard God's call and followed, whether it worked out or not. Why? We have preached at some point about that foolhardy shepherd who left ninety-nine sheep to find just one.

The faithful preacher-administrator also understands the nature of prophetic preaching, and the wisest preacher-administrator even grasps the deep interconnections between prophetic preaching and another peculiar homiletical task, the funeral sermon. At first blush, the funeral, with its somber mood and attempt to comfort the afflicted, seems to swing 180 degrees away from the fiery tone and hellbound effort to afflict the comfortable. But are they really very different? Don't both stand toe to toe with foes that must be identified, exposed, and dethroned? Could it be that the tone of prophetic preaching should, surprisingly enough, be as close as possible to the tone of the funeral homily? And don't both homiletical endeavors fail miserably unless they are of a piece with congregational life, the determination of the people to stare down the daunting foes of death but also injustice, and create a community of love, to do something, to be about the beautiful task of reconciliation? Let us take up the prophetic and then the funeral sermons in turn.

13

The Prophetic

A crucial but often misunderstood aspect of theologically formative preaching is what we usually call the "prophetic." Martin Luther wrote quite powerfully:

> If I profess with the loudest voice and clearest exposition every portion of the truth of God except precisely that little point at which the world and the devil are at that moment attacking, I am not confessing Christ. Where the battle rages, there the loyalty of the soldier is proved.[1]

In my first years of ministry, I felt I had been catapulted out of seminary to fulfill a mission to that little point, to battle the devil on the issues of the day, to prove my loyalty. I was eager to denounce evils of the world and the American economic and military machine, to expose the idols of vacuous religiosity, to poke Jesus into the face of anyone who would listen, rather cocksure I knew the right Christian stance on every controversial political and social issue—"controversial" being the adjective I assume I could lay to rest. I suspect my parishioners viewed me as an angry young man.

But it is never enough for the sermon to be exegetically correct or theologically sound or prophetically pointed. The sermon must strive for beauty. Only beauty can lure us toward God, only beauty is appropriate to God, who is beauty—even when we preach on controversial, political matters. I look back over the many times that I have spoken a strong prophetic word on an issue, boldly declaring steely truth with absolute certainty, yet failing miserably on the score of beauty, never thinking to pick up Orpheus's lyre. Like a rolling panzer, I have fired explosive salvos at a helpless congregation about peace, taking no prisoners, every word iron-plated truth, yet betrayed by a tone and body language that could only be compared to Rambo.

Contrast my powerful words about pacifism to St. Francis, who joined a huge band of Crusaders at Damietta. Armor clinked, sabers rattled, Christians and Muslims staring coldly across no-man's-land, until little Francis, with no chain mail, no battle ax, no shield, barefoot, wearing what today we would call an alb, walked calmly into the teeth of the Muslim line. They drew swords to slaughter him, but such was the novelty of his approach that they took this curiosity to the sultan. Malik al-Kamil and Francis conversed for several days, and the sultan admitted to Francis he would convert to Christianity, but his fellow soldiers would kill him. Francis did buy a brief respite from the combat. A beautiful walk across no-man's-land, a beautiful, gentle sermon, as beautiful as the broken body of Jesus. The preacher can never forget the wisdom of St. Ephrem the Syrian:

> Truth and love are wings that cannot be separated,
> for Truth without Love is unable to fly,
> so too Love without Truth is unable to soar up;
> their yoke is one of harmony.[2]

A harmony of beauty. Truth without beauty cannot fly. The beauty of the Word soars up.

LOVE OF ENEMIES

Preaching a prophetic word is an art, one that tiptoes near the edge of provoking rage but keeps its arms around people who do not understand, who bear visceral feelings that pressure them to push back, who have heard plenty of preaching that buttresses the opposite viewpoint that to them seems holy and good. How do we speak truthfully, while acknowledging the other guy has a good point? How do we, in the preaching moment, engage in a genuine conversation? How do we, in short, love, so that our eyes are not making shrewd observations but shedding love?

To carry on that precarious conversation (while I'm the only one getting to do the talking) requires that I actually have had conversations when others could speak. Partly I can achieve this by reading—not reading books that marshal even stronger arguments for my side, but books that are on the other side, books that I might shun, were it not for the mission of love on which God has set me. But of greatest value is to have real conversations with real people, and to listen more than I talk. If I am going to talk about peace, can I find a veteran or two who got shot at in Vietnam or stormed a beach in Normandy?

Jesus told us to love our enemies. I've preached this often, and a fan of mine once told me I was rather exemplary in loving my enemies: he had seen me having lunch with a rabbi, knew I was tight with African Americans, and saw me on TV with my arm around an imam the evening of 9/11. I blushed at his naïvete, and found myself explaining to him that these people are not my enemies at all. But enemies I do have. My real foes, upon whom I've never expended much love, are my "enemies of thought," people all around me who just think wrong, believe wrong, view the universe wrong.

My neighbor and I smile superficially, sip wine, and chat about the weather, but I seethe at the political sign in his yard and assess him to be a numbskull. I pick up a book, sigh over its flawed reasoning and flat-footed writing, and secretly thank God "that I am not like other men." The clergy in town are worse, preaching vapid, atrocious theology, wrapping themselves in a flag, firing Bible bullets at popular targets. "The Bible is not a weapon!" I have trumpeted, along with my correctly conceived stance that the most important Bible verse in the world right now is "Love your enemies."

As it turns out, I am full of love for *everybody else's* enemies. But for *my* enemies of thought, I harbor violent thoughts. Facing those who believe in violence, I respond with verbal violence. Then it occurs to me that, not only am I utterly inept and uninterested in loving my enemies, but my thought patterns pretty much mirror American foreign policy. I see wrong thinking, and I become unilateral in my thinking, prepared to go it alone because I am right, crushing all foes (even if only in my mind).

Critical thinking is not evil; without making shrewd judgments, we would sink into the kind of life my dog seems to appreciate. I know I am a critic, not just by training, but by nature. As I grow older, my prayer is that God can make me more charitable, hopefully not because my theological brain has suffered evisceration. Nowadays, when I step back and examine my sumptuously informed body of thought, and no matter how skinny the chance that I truly *am* as right as I imagine, I find that my critically addicted soul knows very little joy. I know how to find fault, how to be right, how to zap a foe with the clinching argument, how to marshal one more weighty footnote, and some bizarre pleasure attaches to my rightness of thought. But the joy gets vacuumed out of everything, and I suspect my healing will come only when and if I can learn to love my enemies.

THE LIGHT SHINING

After he retired from serving as a rural mail carrier, my grandfather, Papa Howell, walked me to Mr. Teeter's store, where he joined the other retired men of Oakboro on wooden chairs, chewed tobacco (spitting into a can perilously near my feet), and argued passionately about politics, religion, and society. At the end of the day he went home and then came back the next day to argue some more. These unlettered men knew much about the world and did not settle for half-baked, ingrown opinions, but tested, listened, learned—and loved. My generation does not love enemies of thought. Instead, we are "tolerant," which falls so far short of love as to qualify for a different species altogether. The kind of love that might be faithful to Christ, that might bring me some joy, is *not* that of the clergyman I know who "loves" homosexuals. He is prepared at a moment's notice, should a homosexual happen to show up, to unsheath his scalpel of Bible verses and surgically remove this wickedness, all the while grinning with what he calls the "love of Jesus." There is no Shakespearean "Love alters not" in his ministry, although seeing him reflects back to me what I wish to do to people who brandish flag magnets, support the President "no matter what," believe the poor just need to try harder, and admire Jesus as the prince of capitalism. Doth love alter? or alter not?

Jean Vanier, fully credentialed to speak on such matters, has written,

> To love someone is not first of all to do things for them, but to reveal to them their beauty and value, to say to them through our attitude, "You are beautiful. You are important. I trust you. You can trust yourself." We all know well that we can do things for others and in the process crush them, making them feel that they are incapable of

doing things by themselves. To love someone is to reveal to them their capacities for life, the light that is shining in them.[3]

Can we add "even in the enemy"?

When I preached on the war, I trembled a little when I noticed out in the pew a four-star general who wrote a book on military strategy in Iraq. I asked him to lunch, looked for beauty, noticed his capacity for life and light shining in him. I'd had cross words with a fundamentalist minister across town, an angry dynamo who's trying to rinse sin out of our city. We ate lunch too, swapped child photos, shared dreams and wounds, and I saw more beauty, more light. My neighbor and I started talking about why on earth we think what we think, and in the thicket of craziness I got a glimpse of beauty, definite light. I can't say I have changed my position on this or that. But I find these fledgling lunges at love satisfying. I would swear I even delighted in an unexpected taste of joy just the other day. Maybe it was God saying even to me, "You are beautiful. I trust you. There is light shining in you."

So when I preach on that little point where the battle is raging, do I look for the light, do I grasp the intensity of emotion and embody a robust conversation that might not merely change minds but fashion a bond between hearts?

PROPHECY AND RECONCILIATION

What is the purpose of prophetic preaching? Is it merely to say true things? Or is it the far more daunting task of reconciliation? We are a Church, not a political party; we are not in a winner-take-all contest, but a love-all endeavor. Listen to Vanier exploring the difference between a community of faith and a special-interest group:

> The difference between a community and a group that is only issue-oriented, is that the latter see the enemy outside the group. The struggle is an external one; and there will be a winner and a loser. The group knows it is right and has the truth, and wants to impose it. The members of a community know that the struggle is inside of each person and inside the community; it is against *all* the powers of pride, elitism, hate and depression that are there and which hurt and crush others.[4]

When Jesus said, "Love your enemies," those in earshot had just heard him a few minutes earlier say, "Blessed are the peacemakers," not

"Blessed are the right thinkers about peace." We make peace; God has entrusted to us the ministry of reconciliation, which requires immense humility, a dogged determination to listen, suggest, tantalize, reconsider, and also to act.

Yes, to act. If we dare to speak about an issue, we had best be prepared to mobilize the Body of Christ, and our own bodies, to do something. Whether you can make a case for or against the legal option of abortion, it is hard to gainsay the approach Mother Teresa took when she was awarded the Nobel Peace Prize in 1979. Instead of simply declaiming her viewpoint that abortion is wrong, she pleaded with anyone and everyone: "Give us the child." Being prepared to do something as the Body is the *sine qua non* of preaching on prophetic matters.

While we are acting, we engage in formation. Prophetic preaching is a piece of theological formation, and for it to register, we had best engage in diligent formation on what seem to be nonprophetic issues. Through preaching, through the broader educational program of the Church, we strive over a long period of time to help people come to think theologically. We have a story that we know to be authoritative, but Church folk today do not know how to interact with any story as authoritative. Sam Wells wrote profoundly about the task of prophecy as placing the individual into a larger narrative: "It finds its power precisely in reinvigorating a story that has grown dusty through lack of use. But prophecy is scarcely possible if no story is commonly acknowledged as authoritative. . . . The problem prophecy addresses is not so much evil . . . as forgetfulness."[5]

And so we remember. We remember that Jesus loved his enemies. We relish the delightful truth that Jesus cannot be boxed in as either a liberal Democrat or a conservative Republican, and we dare not let Church members dismiss us as mindless blessers of one or the other angle on how to be an American. We are called to be, as Jim Wallis and Tony Campolo have suggested, "red letter Christians," those whose read of the world and preferred modes of action are taken, not from the cues of politics, but from the red letters, the words of Jesus.[6]

And it is a mistake to think that prophetic preaching is only about big, newsworthy issues. Walter Brueggemann explains the more comprehensive, but more achievable task:

> The task of redescription and subversion is not necessarily or primarily focused on public issues or events. The local crises everywhere around us concerning family and health and jobs—crises that

are the consequences of greed, anxiety, drivenness, loneliness, and violence of systemic proportion—in all of these we come upon the idolatries of society in need of prophetic conversion.[7]

So we begin the conversation with no other goal than to glorify God and to see the Body in action, not changing minds so much as moving the Body together to think, reflect, and embody the ministry of reconciliation that is the true fruit of faithful prophetic preaching.

14

The Funeral

Since we are nearing the end of our book, and since we have contemplated the nature of failure, yet tried to detect its beauty, let us speak briefly of funerals. Little understood and not often explored theologically, the funeral sermon, perhaps more than any other, tests the mettle of the preacher. It either earns her the trust to lead and speak on other matters, or evaporates into trivialities that are an ineffective antidote to the specter of death that looms over all of us.

Many factors—fear of death, pretending death does not really exist, shock at the utter abnormality of death, and the way we insulate ourselves from the dying—not only make preaching the funeral into some patently weird activity, but also may shield Christians from having any sense of the Gospel in the first place. Christianity began with a death; God was glorified in a gruesome execution; Easter happened in a cemetery. Death, a common, normal, expected moment people have understood well enough for all of human history, has been pushed back heroically by modern medicine—but at the price of our denial, our lame inability to think openly, much less robustly, about mortality.

I once heard Allen Verhey[1] describe the way, "once upon a time," people died at home. There were no prolonged medical battles waged in an intensive-care ward. You died at home, and family cared for the dying quite naturally. As death approached, you would hold court in your home as people came by to bid you farewell. To one you might say, "Take care of the chickens for me"; to another, "I forgive you for shooting my cow"; to yet another, "I love you, so be a good boy." But now we die with doctors and immediate family pleading with us to live on—and understandably. In Peter DeVries's moving novel *The Blood of the Lamb*, the father of a dying child is asked by someone in a waiting room why anyone would want to prolong life. His reply? "In order to postpone grief."[2] If you have lived and loved, you may not be patient with those who fuss about the cost of end-of-life treatments or the futility of taking any and all measures to preserve life.

What does it mean theologically to die isolated from community? And without the exchange of words? What does it mean to die clinging to the assumption that death can be still be fended off by just the right medication or procedure? How will we ever parse what Jesus was about if we cannot sing, "Beneath the cross of Jesus I fain would take my stand"?

In such a climate of sheer terror over the prospect of death, in a society where people expect the grieving to "feel better" as soon as possible (and aren't we in the Church complicit in our admiration of those who seem to "move on" with a steely smile?), how is the funeral to be preached? We—every one of us—suffer a curious compulsion to imply one of two theologically bogus notions, and it may be they are two sides to the same counterfeit coin. Many funeral sermons are of the "All dogs go to heaven" variety; if you had a pulse, and if a handful of people loved you enough to show up for your service, you must have been ushered instantly into heaven at the moment of death. Many other funeral sermons are of the "Well done, good and faithful servant" type; he was good, very good, piled up a mountain of good deeds, and God is surely pleased. God is pleased, but where is the grace?

There are multiple preachers in every congregation. The laity utter theological platitudes, especially in the wake of mystery. How often do they say things like, "If anybody deserved to go to heaven, it was Bob"? We have no need to counterpreach in the hallway when we hear this; but in weekly sermons, in the off-the-cuff preaching we do on the sidewalk, and certainly in the funeral sermon, we need to underscore the wonder of grace, to clarify that at least for us who claim to follow Christ, no mountain of good deeds is tall enough, no amassing of grand achievements is even necessary. We are saved by what we all actually crave in our deepest hearts: grace, unearned, unearnable, mind boggling, marvelous.

A PLACE FOR HAGIOGRAPHY

At the same time, there is no reason not to highlight a life well lived. I was trained to avoid eulogy as much as possible and to focus instead on the explication of the text and God's economy of salvation for all people. We need reminders to talk about God in funeral sermons, to work a text, but after we have talked about God, to focus on the Body, the community of faith. If the deceased has exhibited humble service to the needy, the funeral is the perfect time to celebrate that imitation of Christ, to recognize how indispensable such discipleship is to the Body, and even to remind the Body that a hole now exists where the deceased used to be: someone will need to step up now. If the one we grieve has been a great teacher, the funeral is a fitting time to notice how this one taught as Jesus did, to remind us of the importance of wise sages in the life of the Body, and to challenge gently all of us to continue learning and even to dare to teach. Christianity has always highlighted the lives of saints, and there are crafty ways to hold fast to the centrality of grace and the work of Christ in the funeral homily while still honoring the work of the Spirit, the ongoing gift of sanctification, to give thanks and to urge the Church militant to an even higher calling.

Sometimes images begin to emerge as we listen pastorally to families working out the memories and sorrow, images that can dovetail with a text and provide fodder for the funeral sermon. If the deceased loved trees or gardening, instead of simply mentioning this as a self-evidently nice activity, the preacher can craft a sermon around biblical images of trees or plants that can become what Barth called "secular parables" that mirror God's life with us. I once buried a man who was a ferocious card player. I imagined a card game with three players in need of a fourth; most in the congregation that day had been pulled into some game, somewhere, by the deceased. Then I portrayed the Rublev icon of the Trinity—Father, Son, and Holy Spirit—sitting around three sides of a table, with the fourth side open, implying a gentle invitation, that there is room for us to join the holy fellowship that is God.

Sometimes the simplest, least noteworthy life can be the easiest to celebrate in a funeral sermon. Once I buried a man whose family, who clearly loved him dearly, could not think of any memorable moments or funny anecdotes. As we spoke, it occurred to all of us that he was entirely steady, utterly reliable. In the homily I suggested that his lone virtue—and this one virtue is quite enough—was that he kept his promises. When he joined the Church as a boy, he promised to be a member, to learn, and to serve. When he married, he promised to stay married. When he brought his own children for Baptism, he promised to raise them in the Church. Promise keeping is a virtue the Church needs to lift up as exemplary. But there is more, as I recalled from a sermon I had read from Lewis Smedes:

> Yes, somewhere people still make and keep promises. They choose not to quit when the going gets rough. . . . They stick to lost causes. They hold on to a love grown cold. They stay with people who have become pains in the neck. They still dare to make promises and care enough to keep the promises they make. I want to say to you that if you have a ship you will not desert, if you have people you will not forsake, if you have causes you will not abandon, then *you are like God*.[3]

THE WILL OF GOD

Theological consistency is crucial for the ongoing task of formation that is the preaching life, and special care is required around suffering and death. How we counsel, and how we preach in a hospital corridor, may authenticate what we say elsewhere or betray considerable confusion. One day I was summoned to an emergency room, and then I drove frantically with a family to a major medical center two hours away. Their one-year-old daughter had been diagnosed with a terrible malignant tumor in her brain. When doctors swooped her away for exams and initial treatment, I was with the family, and none of us said a word; we cried, but mostly we were just numb. Then another minister walked in, the pastor of some family member, and this pastor was all smiles, all confidence, assuring the family quite confidently that the child would be fine, that God would cure her if we just prayed.

In that moment part of me wished I could be so confident, but my theological perspective is not that if we just pray, God will always shelter us and those we love from harm. In that hour I could not say such a thing, however desperately I wanted to say something to help. When the clergy say such things, it is BS, isn't it? Say anything, say what they want to hear—or perhaps what we as the clergy, ill prepared as we are to grapple with the suffering of a one-year-old, wish to hear. In such moments the preacher is bound only to show up, to draw close to the heart of a family and to the heart of God. The silent presence is more eloquent and far more true than glib words of assurance, which too often prove to be vapid lies. If we lie in such a dire moment, we fritter away any authority we have to speak in the darker moment when God does not save the child.

Perhaps no theological question is more important for the preacher to get right than what is often dubbed "the will of God." A child has a brain tumor, a teenager is killed in a car accident, a mother dies slowly from breast cancer, a man cannot recall the names of his wife or children. Church members will, in their need to say something, utter a half-truth they firmly believe, or sheer BS—like "God took your daughter," or "It was her time," or "God doesn't make mistakes." But by such remarks we build a fatalism into God's people and, more often than we realize, create enemies of God. How many people have we talked to who stopped relating to God years ago because of some tragedy that struck? Before we preach in a weekly pulpit, a hospital waiting room, or a cemetery, we had better figure out that God does not kill children, sow cancer cells in bodies, or hurl one car into another. God is involved, intimately involved, but God is not the doer of evil. Weaving these two theological truths together is the fine art of ministry.

I once presided over the funerals of not one, not two, but three children in a single family. A rare, virulent leukemia was treated three different ways, failing each time. A tumult of grief ensued, and many who knew the family wondered how there could be a God if so much loss were sustained by a single pair of parents. I loved them, and still grieve their deaths; I too felt the *Why?* At the funeral, trying to help friends and family think through such staggering loss, I recalled visiting an old cemetery where I photographed the tombstones of not one or two but three children in a family. Each stone had a profound hymn line etched: "Little ones to him belong; they are weak, but he is strong."

They had died about one hundred years ago, all three from diphtheria. Back then, no one knew what to do about diphtheria, and many children died from it. Science caught up with the disease, and now deaths from diphtheria (at least in the Western world) are rare. One day we will know how to cure (or even prevent) the leukemia that felled my friends. Today we do not know the cure, but if we ask, "Why did they die?" we know the answer to the question. God did not kill them or fail to save them. Bodies break down, disease happens; many sicknesses we can cure, some we will be able to cure but cannot just now. Yet even when we can cure that leukemia, there will be something else, some new disease, something. Funeral sermons can be friendly with modern medicine, but we need to keep a sober distance and dare not heighten the mythology that medicine will (with God as the doctor's helper) finally ensure that we live forever.

And speaking of living forever, how we speak of the afterlife may matter more than we realize. I have heard funeral sermons (and have preached a few myself) that portray heaven as some self-indulgent continuation of a consumer-driven, pleasure-seeking life here on earth. We don't mean any harm if we bury a golfer and say, "Now he's playing that heavenly golf course and getting a birdie on every hole!" When Tammy Faye Baker was nearing death, she told Larry King that heaven would be like a huge shopping mall, and she would have a credit card with no limit. This was a cute comment in a way. But don't we imply by such homiletical drivel that life down here really is about shopping or having fun? Heaven will make us blush, it will be so much fun, the riches will be absurdly lavish, but we might wish to dangle the possibility that eternal life with God will be life with God, about God, devoted to the praise of God. Yes, there will be others in heaven, but not just the people we dig down here! Rather, a dizzying variety of people, the one whose heart we broke eight years ago, the one we despised, the one who hurt us, the ones our prejudice shielded us from even knowing, will be in our fellowship. Heaven will be about God and about the Body. So can the preacher, in weekly preaching and even in the funeral homily, paint a gasping, enthusiastic image of that life God gives that is somehow true, or true enough, before finally falling mute over the wonder that exceeds the best preacher's abilities—and in that gasping failure thereby give God the glory?

OUR OWN FUNERALS

Some preacher—perhaps one who's read this book but maybe not—will stand over your own casket, over you who buried so many and tried to find the words. What will be said in your own funeral homily?

And are we yet alive? When we who are Methodist clergy gather, we customarily open worship by singing this great hymn by Charles Wesley, "And Are We Yet Alive?" We are, but some are not, and we won't be either one day. If we think about clergy and death, we first count it a great privilege to be with people during their darkest hours. A while back a Church member asked, "How do you keep from burning out, dealing with so much suffering and death?" I answered that I may well burn out one day, but not because of dealing with death. If I burn out, it will be because people just can't resist wrangling over some innocuous triviality or another, griping about the coffee or whether the flowers in the Sunday School foyer should be removed on Monday or Tuesday. I will not burn out because I sit by a bedside, or have a grieving spouse or child weeping on my shoulder, or stand by the graveside and watch a granddaughter fight back a tear as she places a flower on her grandfather's casket. It's a privilege; it's why we do what we do.

We get to accompany (and occasionally help) people when they walk through the valley of the shadow of death—but it's always somebody else's death, isn't it? What about when the bell tolls for the preacher? Parishoners probably think clergy are better at facing deaths, the deaths of those they love or even their own, than the laity; but I suspect that, if anything, we are less able to cope. I remember the first minister I ever knew who buried his own wife. Totally desolate, he said, "All that I have preached and believed, the comfort I have tried to give, it seems hollow to me now, it just doesn't help." Perhaps Thomas Merton was right: for us clergy, if some spiritual treasure comes our way, we immediately hand it off to somebody else in counseling or a class or a sermon, and it never has the chance to seep into our own souls. There is a lovely old poem by Sam Shoemaker about where we as ministers find ourselves:

> I stand by the door.
> I neither go too far in, nor stay too far out.
> . . . the door through which men walk when they find God.
> There is no use my going way inside and staying there,
> when so many are still outside.
> . . . .
> Sometimes I take a deeper look in.
> . . . .
> but my place seems closer to the opening.[4]

Have we ever really journeyed inside? The hour of death comes. Can I find my way in? What do I really know about this frontier? Does the doorkeeper of the castle really know the inner rooms? Does the midwife know what being a parent is like?

Years ago, a dear friend, longtime pastor, a titan of ecumenism, a great scholar, a wise mentor, whose friendship I cherished, had just learned at age eighty-nine that he was in his final days. I called, asking to visit. Several family members were there, doing what families do when their father, their husband is dying: milling about, making small talk, not quite looking each other in the eye. I waited for a lull in the conversation and then asked, "They tell me you only have a few days left. How do you feel about that?" He paused, thought, lingered over the silence, and then answered: "When I think about my death, I am . . ." How would he complete the sentence? "I am *curious*." What would death be like? What would the moments after death be like? If you've been a theologian all your life, you can't help being curious about eternity, and God, and the Communion of the Saints. You are curious about what you've understood correctly, and what you have been believing all along that was just plain lunacy. I am curious.

I don't know much of what I wish I knew. At times I trumpet some theological certainty—but is it a professional certainty? or something deeper in me? I don't really know much about death, and cannot pretend I will handle it well at all when it is my own, or if it's my wife who goes first. But while I am curious, I do believe there is a shimmering beauty at the heart of death. Earlier I recounted the day my grandfather died, and haunting beauty in the thick of grief. We all have spoken with countless parishioners who have counted it an immense privilege to be with loved ones when they breathed their last, and the surprising loveliness of the moment.

Death is beautiful, because the death of Jesus, our brother and our Lord, is beautiful: Jesus, his perfect body, all loving, all holy, nailed to an olive shaft that must have trembled with all of nature under the weight of his sacrifice, his blood poured out, sorrow and love flow mingled down, the water from his side, the river that makes glad the city of God, the healing of the nations, a window thrown open into the very heart of God, the turning point of history, the light that banishes every darkness.

While we have been guilty of trivializing heaven in our funeral sermons, we may struggle to envision a truer heaven for ourselves. There's an old joke pastors have circulated that you might have heard. Two clergy meet in the afterlife. One says, "Hey, compared to parish ministry, heaven is great!" And the other minister says, "Uh, this isn't heaven." Parish ministry is hard, and disappointing in many ways. We have spoken of failure, and our failure may become the window to grace for us who preach as we draw inexorably closer to our own deaths.

Disappointment? Look back over your ministry, and you discover you have been drifting into a kind of oblivion that starts way sooner than we care to admit. I ran into a man who told me he was a member of a Church I had once served. I said, "Cool: I used to be the minister there." He looked puzzled and asked, "What's your name?" "James

Howell." He squinted a little and said, "I think maybe I've heard some-body mention your name, I don't know . . ." I smiled pleasantly and restrained myself from saying, "I poured twelve years of my life, heart, soul, and blood into that Church, and I've been gone only four years!"

You know how it goes: you go back for a homecoming, you notice your photograph in the gallery of rogues in the hallway. People are mildly happy to see you—but then they dive into the pork and beans and fried chicken, chattering about whatever is more current in their life than you, the old fossil. Oblivion. A few more years, and no one will remember us. Just one picture on the wall among many.

I had intended, we all had intended to leave some profound mark on the Church, never to be forgotten. I longed to be a modern day John Chrysostom, a fiery prophetic force that would change the world. But I drift, you drift, we all drift into certain oblivion—and this is not a bad thing. I used to test out as an extrovert, one of those people who draws great energy from being around people. But as I get older, I find they wear me out, they drain energy. I think I actually love them more, but at the same time I'm becoming more content to sit on the rocking chair on the back porch.

We are drifting toward oblivion, toward being *lost in wonder, love, and praise*. As a clergyperson down here, you have to be a single voice, and it gets lonely lots of days. Knowing our one voice will be forgotten, we leave it behind: take care of my chickens; take care of my church. Then we walk through the door—the way an individual grape or a single grain of wheat drifts into the oblivion of a cask of wine and a loaf of bread, and on the table becomes the body and blood of our Lord. Or the way a small drop of water, a tear, or the mist, joins an innumer-able host of other droplets of water, and I become part of a cloud, just a drop in a cloud of witnesses, and it is at the very end of the day, as the sun returns to its resting place, that the drops, the cloud, refracts the light of the sun and multiplies itself into stunning hues, a dazzling dance of stunning color, the glory of God almighty, the beauty we know only as darkness descends.

Conclusion

15

The Preaching Self

Until that day when we are spoken of—hopefully well, since we will have no chance to reply!—how do we live? Does the life of the preacher matter? It must; but what is this life like? Barth said we may be "hopeful but not happy,"[1] and I find myself wanting to argue with him, although I suspect I would lose and wind up testifying for the hopeful unhappiness of the ministerial life.

The very subject of homiletics is often, to me and I would imagine to many others, strangely demoralizing. The legends of preaching may not inspire us so much as dwarf our puny efforts. Twenty thousand pressed onto Boston Common to hear George Whitefield, and even cynical old Benjamin Franklin admitted that, on hearing the "grand itinerant," he emptied his pockets. John Chrysostom, with piercing eyes and penetrating voice, preached brilliantly and even irritatingly on the moral claims of Scripture; mesmerized audiences burst into thunderous applause, riots broke out, and the empress forced him into exile in Armenia. Frederick Douglass was so awestruck by Sojourner Truth that he stammered, "We were all for a moment brought to a standstill, just as we should have been if someone had thrown a brick through the window."[2] There is that great admonition from Henry Ward Beecher:

> To preach the Gospel of Jesus Christ; to have Christ so melted and dissolved in you that when you preach your own self you preach Him as Paul did; to have every part of you living and luminous with Christ,

and then to make use of everything that is in you, your analogical reasoning, your imagination, your mirthfulness, your humor, your indignation, your wrath; to take everything that is in you all steeped in Jesus Christ, and to throw yourself with all your power upon a congregation—that has been my theory of preaching the Gospel.[3]

I so very desperately want Christ to be melted and dissolved in me, but I simply have never been able to muster anything resembling a me that is "all steeped in Jesus Christ." But maybe, whatever my foibles, I can at least exhibit an earnest longing for Christ to be melted in me. Maybe, whatever my failures, when I step gingerly into the pulpit, my parishioners at least might glimpse some evidence of a determined if flawed response to God's calling.

HOW BEAUTIFUL THE FEET

Writing to a small band of Christians in Rome who had never laid eyes on him, the apostle Paul got on a rant about the importance of preaching, with a proof text from Isaiah 52: "How beautiful are the feet of those who preach good news!" (Rom. 10:15). Was he looking down? Were his feet sore, as we might suspect of someone who walked all over the hilly, rocky countries we call Turkey, Greece, Lebanon, and Israel?

Statues in Western Christendom depict Paul as balding, bearded, wielding a ridiculously large sword. The earliest, tantalizing portrait of Paul was penned a century after his death: *The Acts of Paul* stated he was "a man of small stature, with a bald head and crooked legs, eyebrows meeting and nose somewhat hooked," but with "the face of an angel."[4] Except for the face, this description reminds me of Gollum, the quirky, wrinkled, downright ugly creature who leads Frodo and Sam to Mordor in *The Lord of the Rings*, his feet crusty, calloused, almost painful to look at.

The preacher's feet nowadays are well-hidden, covered by socks and shoes, shielded by a pulpit or obscured by sight lines. Isaiah and Paul weren't remarking on the aesthetic loveliness of feet; the point was that they moved, they went, they propped up the one preaching. A child sings, "Little feet, where have you been?" My podiatrical report tells a lot about who I am. In a shimmering scene in *Soldier of the Great War*, Mark Helprin tells of a wily old World War I veteran out walking the backroads of Italy. Joined by a young man who complains of fatigue, the elderly Alessandro declares,

You may be tall, handsome, intelligent and gifted; but if you have feet of despair you might as well shine shoes on the Via del Corso; feet of despair are too tender, can't fight back. Under prolonged assault they come apart and bleed to death; they become infected and swollen in half an hour. On the other hand are feet of invincibility. Feet of invincibility are ugly, but they last forever—building defenses where they are attacked, turning color, reproportioning and repositioning themselves until they look like bulldogs.[5]

The feet are exhibit A in the person of the preacher. Who are you? Who are we, whose feet walk out of the normalcy of life in the world, through seminary corridors and library stacks, then step up into pulpits? Are we weary and blistered a bit? Ugly but dogged?

I saw on television a physically handicapped woman who actually paints with her feet. "How beautiful are the feet of those who preach good news." The preacher is a painter of sorts, with a brush not only of mouth but also body; what comes out on the canvas of the sermon is not even the words and bodily movements, but what they reveal (and simultaneously what they hide), the self of the preacher. We might prefer the self to get out of the way, but it's just there, nobody can miss it—not the preacher, not the choir, not the person on the back pew. We can only pray that God somehow multiplies the measly loaves and fishes of a small soul, through their tangible offering, and the feet somehow become beautiful, and the good news is heard.

We can also work on the self, and understand how the self can be the rich soil in which a sermon can grow, or the rocky terrain in which seeds sprout only briefly but then wither. A primary question we can't help asking our selves about our selves is one of faith. Do we really believe what we are preaching? We need not be ultra-pious, we need not be the kind of pure, true believer who never harbors a glimmer of doubt, we need not be entirely orthodox or nearing perfection in holiness. But is there something like belief, and is it evident?

HAIR ON FIRE

One of the young associate pastors with whom I had the delight of working showed up at our parish, fresh out of seminary, determined to herd two thousand people rather unwillingly to oppose the death penalty, to welcome gays into the Church, and perhaps even to dismantle the military machine of the United States along the way: not political liberalism, but a deadly serious read of the Gospel and its implications for today. His approach wasn't slick or well calculated, and actually dozens in our parish were angrily annoyed by him. An older business executive offered to send him to some management school and to a speech coach, which would certainly smooth out the rough edges. Another warned me, "You'd better rein in that new associate." I told them both we'd ruin him if we did. When his time on our staff had ended, a respectable number of archconservatives one by one dropped by my office to declare that they missed him, and that he had compelled them to rethink quite a few things. All he had going for him was quite enough: he really believed.

A few years later, another young associate landed in a different parish with me. She sprinted up and down the halls, late for appointments, hair on fire—and in a pretty genteel, culturally elevated kind of place. A few voiced concern about her professionalism or time management. But she was generally rushing in or out of the building because her heart was clearly out of the building, over across the railroad tracks, with the poor, whom she rather oddly didn't think of as charity cases but as friends, not as objects for our pity but as fellow siblings in the family of God. She could not tell you her leadership style, and most leadership gurus would want to send her off to a workshop or three. But gradually people started rushing around behind her, next to her, showing up late for meetings, hair on fire, spending more and more time out of the building, befriending former charity cases. She was a believer, and it was never about *her*.

MUST WE BE HOLY?

She was also holy. Must the preacher be holy? St. Athanasius is often quoted on this, but we could select any of the great theologians through history and they would concur:

> For the searching and right understanding of the Scriptures there is need of a good life and a pure soul, and for Christian virtue to guide the mind to grasp, so far as human nature can, the truth concerning God the Word. One cannot possibly understand the teaching of the saints unless one has a pure mind and is trying to imitate their life. Anyone who wishes to understand the mind of the sacred writers must . . . approach the saints by copying their deeds.[6]

One medieval biographer characterized the preaching of St. Francis:

> Not with enticing words of human wisdom, but in the doctrine and
> virtue of the Holy Spirit he proclaimed the Kingdom of God with
> great confidence; as a true preacher, he never used flattering words
> and he despised all blandishments; what he preached to others in
> words, he had first experienced by deeds, so that he might speak the
> truth faithfully.[7]

Talk about pressure. I have to be saintly to preach?

Think about Peter Shaffer's play *Amadeus* or the film version. Salieri
is a court composer, zealously pious, offering his music entirely to God.
But it is the impious, sophomoric, unholy Mozart whose music is truly
beautiful. Salieri, dumbfounded with admiration, admits, "This was
a music I had never heard, filled with such longing, such unfulfillable
longing. It seemed to me that I was hearing the voice of God." Could it
be that the holy, no matter how fervently we recommend holiness, acci-
dentally seal themselves from the real world, the one that God made
and came to reconcile to God's own self, and thereby miss the under-
tones, the depth, the heartbreaking wrinkle, the sheer delight?

Michelangelo once said that an artist "must maintain a good life,
and if possible be holy, so that his intellect can be inspired by the Holy
Spirit."[8] And so his intellect was. But Caravaggio, in his lifetime better
known for drunkenness and brawling than painting, depicted Christ
in a way that led Desmond Seward to conclude that "Despite being
a rebel by temperament, he was passionately orthodox in his religious
beliefs. . . . always his grasp of theology was impeccable."[9] Why is it
God can use individuals of intense inner turmoil (Luther?) and even
suspect private lives? The reason is that it is God, of course.

Could it be that, instead of juggling the relative virtues of holiness or an earthier tendency, we might simply realize how crucial it is
for the preacher to be immersed in the real world? We could choose
countless mentors for such an enterprise; for now let us think of
Johnny Cash as a mental model for preaching. When I was a boy, my
dad admired Johnny Cash, but I scoffed, joking that even when Cash
talks (which happens often in his songs) he is off-key. But lie back in
your lounger, drink some cheap beer, and listen to him. Garbled amid
that gravelly voice are lyrics that are raw, seeping out from behind a
dark life, ranging with us behind bars, the rhythm of the chain gang,
an intrepid trudging through a hard life, one step weighted by sorrow

that couldn't stay in pitch if it had to, the next step surprisingly taken, as if some unexpected momentum lunges forward, forward toward some hope that isn't sunny optimism but hard-won, gritty determination. The preacher needs no sonorous vocal ability, no Churchillian verbiage, but rather a brutal honesty that has paid sensitive, strong attention to life down here, fallen as it may be; instead of merely telling people how they ought to feel, the preacher needs to begin by naming how they in fact do feel.

Then, and only then, can we make a connection between the hard, brute facts of life and the reality of God. We need not tie up every problem with a pretty bow of an answer, but we can stammer a bit and offer feeble but palpable evidence that there is a God in the thick of life. To get there in even tentative fashion, we go deep into the Scriptures, deep into the world, and deep into our selves, the selves God made and called to preach. In Ann Patchett's novel *Bel Canto*, a man is taken, awestruck, annihilated in his soul by a woman singing:

> Never had he thought, never once, that such a woman existed, one who stood so close to God that God's own voice poured from her. How far she must have gone inside herself to call up that voice. It was as if the voice came from the center part of the earth and by the sheer effort and diligence of her will she had pulled it up through the dirt and rock and through the floorboards of the house, up into her feet, where it pulled through her, reaching, lifting, warmed by her, and then out of the white lily of her throat and straight to God in heaven. It was a miracle and he wept for the gift of bearing witness.[10]

How far into ourselves can we go?

WORN SMALL ROCK

We go then not only into ourselves but into the life of the Body. A few years ago someone pointed me to a stunning passage in William Faulkner's *The Sound and the Fury*. The whole novel is a marvel, but his pitch perfect portrayal of a single preacher, the pastor of the maid of the affluent Dilsey family, is frankly my ideal for who I want to be when I grow up as a preacher.

Faulkner describes his voice as having "sad, timbrous quality." He walked back and forth,

a meager figure, hunched over upon itself like that of one long
immured in striving with the implacable earth. . . . He was like a
worn small rock whelmed by the successive waves of his voice. . .
The congregation seemed to watch with its own eyes while the voice
consumed him, until he was nothing and they were nothing and
there was not even a voice but instead their hearts were speaking to
one another in chanting measures beyond the need for words, so
that . . . a long moaning expulsion of breath rose from them, and a
woman's single soprano: "Yes, Jesus!"[11]

I do not know how to conduct a workshop, or how to write a book,
or even how to try for myself on how to become such a worn, small
rock. I do feel worn and small—and perhaps it was to such a worn,
shabby, and insignificant Simon Peter that Jesus said, "On this rock
I will build my church." At the end it's not about the preacher or the
sermons but the hearts of the people speaking to one another until he
is nothing and they are nothing and it is all God. Perhaps if you and
I read Faulkner's quite stunning vision now and then, we will in our
failure become a cipher into the very heart of God.

I conclude with another moment from my own reading, reading
that does not so much supply me with preaching material, but pulls
back the veil on my life and work, and I begin to understand. Consider
Gail Godwin's marvelous assessment of the words of one aging pastor,
Father Gower, that in the novel were spoken to the young woman who
indeed was *Father Melancholy's Daughter*:

He's not trendy; he doesn't pose. He's neither a self-transcendent
guru nor one of these fund-raising manager types who have become
so sought after lately by our Holy Church. He's just himself—
himself offered daily. He worries about people, he worries about
himself. . . . He goes to the hospital carrying the Sacraments in his
little black case. He baptizes and marries and buries and listens to
people's fears and confessions and isn't above sharing some of his
own. He scrubs the corner cross with Ajax. His sermons have real
substance; you can tell he wrestled them into shape with his whole
mind—and he delivers them with conviction. He makes his services
beautiful; he reminds you that the whole purpose of the liturgy is
to put you in touch with the great rhythms of life. He's a dedicated
man, your father. He's lonely and bedeviled like the rest of us, but
he has time for it all and tries to do it right. He lives by the grace of

daily obligation. He's what the priests in books used to be like, but today he's a rarity.[12]

Melancholy he has every right to be, as do you and I. He is not happy, but supremely hopeful; he suffers an inability, and yet bears the obligation to preach, and through his ministry, the beautiful song is overheard, from off in the distance someplace, luring all of us home.

Notes

Chapter 1: Obligation and Inability

1. Karl Barth, *The Word of God and the Word of Man*, trans. Douglas Horton (New York: Harper & Row, 1957), 186.

2. Michael P. Knowles, *We Preach Not Ourselves: Paul on Proclamation* (Grand Rapids: Brazos Press, 2008), 17.

3. Gail Godwin, *Father Melancholy's Daughter* (New York: William Morrow & Co., 1991), 225.

4. Walter Brueggemann, *The Word Militant: Preaching a Decentering Word* (Minneapolis: Fortress Press, 2007), 125.

5. Taylor Branch, *Parting the Waters: America in the King Years, 1954–63* (New York: Simon & Schuster, 1988), 99.

6. Augustine, *On Christian Doctrine*, trans. D. W. Robertson (Indianapolis: Bobbs-Merrill, 1958), 142.

7. Elaine Scarry, *On Beauty and Being Just* (Princeton, NJ: Princeton University Press, 1999), 27.

8. St. Augustine, *Works of Saint Augustine: Sermons*, vol. 2, trans. Edmund Hill, ed. John E. Rotelle (Brooklyn: New City Press, 1990), 107.

9. Stanley Hauerwas, *Performing the Faith: Bonhoeffer and the Practice of Nonviolence* (Grand Rapids: Brazos Press, 2004), 164.

Chapter 2: What to Talk About

1. Adam Gopnik, *Angels and Ages: A Short Book about Darwin, Lincoln and Modern Life* (New York: Knopf, 2009), 17f, 22.

2. Thomas Merton, *The Seven-Storey Mountain* (New York: Harcourt Brace Jovanovich), 73.

3. Dietrich Bonhoeffer, *Letters and Papers from Prison*, ed. Eberhard Bethge (New York: Macmillan, 1971), 156f.

4. Elizabeth von Arnim, *The Enchanted April* (New York: New York Review Books, 2007), 55f.

Chapter 3: How Texts Work

1. Thomas Long has written wisely on this issue in *Preaching and the Literary Forms of the Bible* (Philadelphia: Fortress Press, 1989).

2. Alyce McKenzie, *Preaching Proverbs: Wisdom for the Pulpit* (Louisville, KY: Westminster John Knox Press, 1996).

3. Alan Paton, *Cry the Beloved Country* (New York: Collier Books, 1987), 124.

4. Robert Jenson, *Systematic Theology,* vol. 1, *The Triune God* (New York: Oxford University Press, 1997), 173.

5. C. S. Lewis, "The Weight of Glory," in *The Weight of Glory,* ed. Walter Hooper (New York: HarperCollins, 2001), 26.

6. See J. Clinton McCann Jr. and James C. Howell, *Preaching the Psalms* (Nashville: Abingdon Press, 2001).

7. Garrett Greene, *Imagining God: Theology and the Religious Imagination* (San Francisco: Harper & Row, 1989), 83.

8. Augustine, *On Christian Doctrine,* II.6, trans. D. W. Robertson (Indianapolis: Bobbs-Merrill, 1958), 37.

9. J. R. R. Tolkien, *The Two Towers* (New York: Ballantine, 1954), 80.

10. Thucydides, *The Peloponnesian War,* 3.82.4.

11. Robert Jay Lifton, *Nazi Doctors: Medical Killing and the Psychology of Genocide* (New York: Basic Books, 2000), 202.

12. C. H. Spurgeon, *The Treasury of David,* vol. I (Peabody, MA: Hendrickson, 1988), 153.

Chapter 4: Ranking the Subjects

1. Karl Barth, *The Word of God and the Word of Man* (New York: Harper & Row, 1957), 195.

2. C. S. Lewis, "The Weight of Glory," in *The Weight of Glory,* ed. Walter Hooper (New York: HarperCollins, 2001), 25–46.

3. Samuel Wells, *Speaking the Truth: Preaching in a Pluralistic Culture* (Nashville: Abingdon Press, 2008), 10.

4. Harry Emerson Fosdick, "What Is the Matter with Preaching?" *Harper's Magazine* (July 1928), 133–41, reprinted and discussed now in Mike Graves, ed., *What's the Matter with Preaching Today?* (Louisville, KY: Westminster John Knox Press, 2004), 8.

5. Dietrich Bonhoeffer, *Letters and Papers from Prison,* ed. Eberhard Bethge (New York: Macmillan, 1971), 361.

6. Jason Byassee, *Praise Seeking Understanding: Reading the Psalms with Augustine* (Grand Rapids: Eerdmans, 2007), 103.

7. Hans Urs von Balthasar, *The Balthasar Reader,* ed. Medard Kehl and Werner Löser, trans. Robert J. Daly and Fred Lawrence (New York: Crossroad, 1997), 431.

8. Karl Barth, *The Epistle to the Romans,* trans. E. C. Hoskyns (New York: Oxford University Press, 1968), 7.

9. William H. Willimon, *Conversations with Barth on Preaching* (Nashville: Abingdon Press, 2006), 79.

Chapter 5: How to Tell the Truth

1. Phillips Brooks, "The Congregation," in *The Company of Preachers: Wisdom on Preaching, Augustine to the Present*, ed. Richard Lischer (Grand Rapids: Eerdmans, 2002), 393.

2. Karl Barth, *Homiletics*, trans. Geoffrey W. Bromiley and Donald E. Daniels (Louisville, KY: Westminster/John Knox Press, 1991), 118f.

3. The language of "coherence" and "contingency" is wisely explicated in J. Christiaan Beker, *Paul the Apostle: The Triumph of God in Life and Thought* (Philadelphia: Fortress Press, 1980).

4. Annie Dillard, *The Writing Life* (New York: HarperPerennial, 1989), 72.

5. Harry G. Frankfurt, *On Bullshit* (Princeton, NJ: Princeton University Press, 2005).

6. Mark Helprin, *Winter's Tale* (New York: Pocket, 1983), 211.

7. Bob Pierce, quoted in Richard Stearns, *The Hole in Our Gospel: What Does God Expect of Us?* (Nashville: Thomas Nelson, 2009), 109.

8. Frederick Buechner, *The Magnificent Defeat* (San Francisco: Harper & Row, 1966), 10–18.

9. Karl Barth, *Church Dogmatics*, III/3, trans. G. W. Bromiley and R. J. Ehrlich (Edinburgh: T. & T. Clark, 1960), 295f.

Chapter 6: Out Loud and Out There

1. Jürgen Moltmann, *The Church in the Power of the Spirit*, trans. Margaret Kohl (Minneapolis: Fortress Press, 1993), 207.

2. David C. Steinmetz, *Luther and Staupitz* (Durham, NC: Duke University Press, 1980), 57.

3. David Halberstam, *Summer of '49* (New York: Avon Books, 1989), 163.

4. Halberstam, *Summer of '49*, 158–59.

5. Rowan Williams, *A Ray of Darkness: Sermons and Reflections* (Cambridge, MA: Cowley Publications, 1995), 3.

6. Hans-Georg Gadamer, *The Relevance of the Beautiful and Other Essays*, trans. Nicholas Walker (Cambridge: Cambridge University Press, 1986), 67.

7. Rainer Maria Rilke, *Duino Elegies*, trans. Edward Snow (New York: North Point, 2000), 5.

8. J. R. R. Tolkien, *The Fellowship of the Ring* (New York: Ballantine, 1955), 298.

9. Pascal Bonafoux, *Van Gogh: The Passionate Eye* (New York: Harry N. Abrams, 1987), 41.

10. Annie Dillard, *Pilgrim at Tinker Creek* (New York: HarperCollins, 1974), 8. Later she adds, "I cannot cause light; the most I can do is try to put myself in the path of its beam" (p. 33).

11. Dillard, *Pilgrim at Tinker Creek*, 14–15.

12. Frederick Buechner, *The Sacred Journey* (San Francisco: HarperSanFrancisco, 1982), 6.

13. Buechner, *The Sacred Journey*, 6f.

Chapter 7: Secular Parables and Saints

1. Charles Haddon Spurgeon, *Lectures to My Students* (Grand Rapids: Baker, 1977), 1–2.

2. Karl Barth, *Church Dogmatics*, IV/3, trans. G. W. Bromiley and T. F. Torrance (Edinburgh: T. & T. Clark, 1961), 111. A nice discussion of these secular parables may be found in George Hunsinger, *How to Read Karl Barth: The Shape of His Theology* (New York: Oxford University Press, 1991), 234–80.

3. Barth, *CD* IV/3: 112–13.

4. Barth, *CD* IV/3: 115.

5. Frederick Buechner, *The Sacred Journey* (San Francisco: HarperSanFrancisco, 1982), 1–2.

6. John Navone, *Enjoying God's Beauty* (Collegeville, MN: Liturgical Press, 1999), xiii. Later he writes, "Beauty is the power of good to draw us toward excellence" (9).

7. Pascal Bonafoux, *Van Gogh: The Passionate Eye* (New York: Harry N. Abrams, 2001), 135.

8. G. K. Chesterton, *St. Francis of Assisi* (Garden City, NY: Image, 1957), 117–18.

9. Jim Forest, *Love Is the Measure: A Biography of Dorothy Day*, rev. ed. (Maryknoll, NY: Orbis Books, 1994), 59.

10. Edith Wyschogrod, *Saints and Postmodernism: Revisioning Moral Philosophy* (Chicago: University of Chicago Press, 1990), 13.

Chapter 8: Delivery

1. Barbara Brown Taylor, *The Preaching Life* (Cambridge, MA: Cowley Publications, 1993), 78.

2. Rainer Maria Rilke, *Letters to a Young Poet*, trans. M. D. Herter Norton (New York: W. W. Norton & Co., 1934), 72.

3. William Manchester, *The Last Lion: Winston Spencer Churchill, Visions of Glory* (Boston: Dell, 1984), 33.

4. Hans-Georg Gadamer, *The Relevance of the Beautiful and Other Essays*, trans. Nicholas Walker (Cambridge: Cambridge University Press, 1987), 79.

5. Michael Erard, *Um . . . : Slips, Stumbles, and Verbal Blunders, and What They Mean* (New York: Anchor, 2008).

6. T. S. Eliot, "Four Quartets," *Collected Poems, 1909–1962* (New York: Harcourt Brace Jovanovich, 1963), 189.

7. Eudora Welty, *The Optimist's Daughter* (New York: Vintage Books, 1968), 140.

8. Gadamer, *The Relevance of the Beautiful*, 84.

9. George Eliot, *Adam Bede* (New York: Penguin, 1961), 34ff.

10. Maynard Solomon, *Mozart: A Life* (New York: HarperPerennial, 1995), 115, 118.

Chapter 9: Aftermath

1. Frederick Buechner, *Telling the Truth: The Gospel as Tragedy, Comedy and Fairy Tale* (New York: Harper & Row, 1977), 22–23.

2. Heimito von Doderer, quoted in David James Duncan, *The Brothers K* (New York: Bantam, 1993), 333.

3. Richard Lischer, *Open Secrets: A Memoir of Faith and Discovery* (New York: Broadway, 2001), 76.

4. Arthur Miller, *After the Fall: A Play in Two Acts* (New York: Penguin Books, 1964), 4.

5. Martin Luther, quoted in O. C. Edwards Jr., *A History of Preaching* (Nashville: Abingdon Press, 2004), 287–88.

6. Dio Chrysostom, quoted in Michael P. Knowles, *We Preach Not Ourselves: Paul on Proclamation* (Grand Rapids: Brazos Press, 2008), 28.

7. Joseph Sittler, *Gravity and Grace* (Minneapolis: Augsburg Publishing House, 1986), 63.

8. T. H. L. Parker, *The Oracles of God: An Introduction to the Preaching of John Calvin* (Cambridge: Lutterworth, 2002).

9. Roland H. Bainton, *Here I Stand: A Life of Martin Luther* (New York: Abingdon-Cokesbury Press, 1950), 82.

10. Frank Darabont, Stephen King, *The Shawshank Redemption: The Shooting Script* (New York: Newmarket, 1996), 63–64.

11. Richard Lischer, *The End of Words: The Language of Reconciliation in a Culture of Violence* (Grand Rapids: Eerdmans, 2005), 8.

Chapter 10: Failure

1. T. S. Eliot, "Four Quartets," *Collected Poems, 1909–1962* (New York: Harcourt Brace Jovanovich, 1963), 189.

2. Thomas Merton, "Letter to a Young Activist," in *The Hidden Ground of Love* (New York: Farrar, Straus & Giroux, 1985).

Chapter 11: Preaching and Administration

1. Nicholas Lash, "Human Experience and the Knowledge of God," in *Theology on the Way to Emmaus* (London: SCM Press, 1986), 141–57.

2. Jim Collins, *Good to Great: Why Some Companies Make the Leap . . . and Others Don't* (New York: HarperBusiness, 2001), 74–75.

3. Marianne Williamson, as heard by Anne Lamott, *Bird by Bird: Some Instructions on Writing and Life* (New York: Anchor, 1994), 167.

4. George MacDonald, cited by C. S. Lewis, *Mere Christianity* (New York: Macmillan, 1943), 174.

5. Ronald Heifetz, *Leadership without Easy Answers* (Cambridge, MA: Harvard University Press, 1998), 241.

6. Collins, *Good to Great*, 13.

7. Collins, *Good to Great*, 186.

Chapter 12: Preaching and Theological Formation

1. Gail Godwin, *Father Melancholy's Daughter* (New York: William Morrow & Co., 1991), 225.

2. The material we used and the sermons I preached can be found in *The Life We Claim: The Apostles' Creed in Preaching, Teaching and Worship* (Nashville: Abingdon Press, 2005).

3. Godwin, *Father Melancholy's Daughter*, 225.

Chapter 13: The Prophetic

1. Martin Luther, *Letters*, vol. 3, 81

2. Sebastian Brock, *The Luminous Eye: The Spiritual World Vision of Saint Ephrem* (Kalamazoo, MI: Cistercian, 1985), 45.

3. Jean Vanier, *From Brokenness to Community* (New York: Paulist Press, 1992), 16.

4. Jean Vanier, *Community and Growth*, rev. ed. (New York: Paulist Press, 1989), 29–30.

5. Samuel Wells, *Speaking the Truth: Preaching in a Pluralistic Culture* (Nashville: Abingdon Press, 2008), 5–6.

6. Tony Campolo, *Red Letter Christians: A Citizen's Guide to Faith and Politics* (Ventura, CA: Regal, 2008).

7. Walter Brueggemann, *The Word Militant: Preaching a Decentering Word* (Minneapolis: Fortress Press, 2007), 18.

Chapter 14: The Funeral

1. On the way the dying are alienated from community, see Allen Verhey, *Reading the Bible in the Strange World of Medicine* (Grand Rapids: Eerdmans, 2003), 336–44.

2. Peter DeVries, *The Blood of the Lamb* (New York: Popular, 1961), 179.

3. Lewis B. Smedes, "The Power of Promises," in *A Chorus of Witnesses: Model Sermons for Today's Preacher*, ed. Thomas G. Long and Cornelius Plantinga Jr. (Grand Rapids: Eerdmans, 1994), 156.

4. Samuel Moor Shoemaker, "I Stand by the Door," in *I Stand by the Door* (Waco: Word, 1967).

Chapter 15: The Preaching Self

1. Karl Barth, *The Word of God and the Word of Man*, trans. Douglas Horton (New York: Harper & Row, 1957), 183.

2. Nell Irvin Painter, *Sojourner Truth: A Life, A Symbol* (New York: W. W. Norton, 1996), 161.

3. Debby Applegate, *The Most Famous Man in America: The Biography of Henry Ward Beecher* (New York: Doubleday, 2006), 274.

4. "The Acts of Paul," in *New Testament Apocrypha*, vol. 2, ed. E. Hennecke et al. (Philadelphia: Westminster Press, 1965), 353f.

5. Mark Helprin, *Soldier of the Great War* (New York: Avon, 1991), 18.

6. Athanasius, *On the Incarnation* (Crestwood: St. Vladimir's, 1953), 96.

7. Giovanni di Ceprano, *St. Francis of Assisi, The Little Flowers, Legends and Lauds*, ed. Otto Karrer, trans. N. Wydenbruck (London: Sheed and Ward, 1947), 27.

8. James H. Beck, *Three Worlds of Michelangelo* (New York: W. W. Norton, 1999), 3.

9. Desmond Seward, *Caravaggio: A Passionate Life* (New York: William Morrow & Co., 1998), 67, 73.

10. Ann Patchett, *Bel Canto* (New York: Perennial, 2001), 54.

11. William Faulkner, *The Sound and the Fury* (New York: W. W. Norton & Co., 1994), 183.

12. Gail Godwin, *Father Melancholy's Daughter* (New York: William Morrow & Co.), 199.

Index